874

YORK

General Editors Professor A.N. Jeffares (University of Stirling) & Professor Suheil Bushrui (*American University of Beirut*)

Thomas Hardy

TESS OF THE D'URBERVILLES

Notes by David Lindley

MA B PHIL (OXFORD)
Lecturer in English Literature, University of Leeds

LONGMAN
YORK PRESS

D0416248

HARROGATE COLLEGE OF ARTS
AND TECHNOLOGY LIBRARY

CLASS 823.8 HAR

ACCESS No. 01.939

DATE 7/2/95 LOCATION H

LEEDS METROPOLITAN
UNIVERSITY LIBRARY

17 0253406 X

823.8 HAR

YORK PRESS
Immeuble Esseily, Place Riad Solh, Beirut.

LONGMAN GROUP LIMITED
Longman House, Burnt Mill,
Harlow, Essex CM20 2JE, England
and Associated Companies throughout the World.

© Librairie du Liban 1980

*All rights reserved. No part of this publication may be reproduced,
stored in a retrieval system, or transmitted in any form or by any
means, electronic, mechanical, photocopying, recording, or otherwise,
without the prior permission of the copyright owner.*

First published 1980
Second impression 1984
Third impression 1986
ISBN 0 582 78094 2
Produced by Longman Group (FE) Ltd
Printed in Hong Kong

Contents

Part 1

Introduction

Hardy's life

Thomas Hardy was born on 2 June 1840 in the tiny hamlet of Upper Bockhampton in the county of Dorset. His mother came from a very poor family, and though his father, a master mason with men working for him, was better off than many in the area, the Hardy family were in the eyes of Victorian society little better than peasants.

Hardy owed a great deal to his parents. From his father, who had played for many years in the small band which accompanied services at the parish church, and who was often asked to play his violin for local festivities, Hardy gained a love of music. As a young boy he himself played at dances, experience which finds its way into the descriptions of country celebrations in *Tess* and elsewhere. Hardy's mother was an even greater influence. From his earliest years she encouraged her son to read widely; she saw to it that he went to the very best local schools, where he had a good basic education, even, unusually, learning Latin and French. Moreover Hardy learnt from her many of the country legends which colour all his work, and she helped to foster the strong sense of the past which forms one of the deepest strands in his imagination.

After leaving school at the age of sixteen, Hardy was apprenticed to a local architect, John Hicks, thus moving up the social scale from craft to profession. He worked conscientiously at the job, as at everything he ever did, while still finding time to carry on his private reading, extending his studies to include learning Greek. He moved to another architect's office in London from 1862–7, where, for the first time, he was able to visit theatres, concert halls and art galleries, all of which made a deep impression upon him. It was at this period that he began to write poetry, though none was published.

On returning to Dorset in 1867 he wrote a novel, *The Poor Man and the Lady*. Though this work was not published (and does not survive) the kind opinions offered by those who read it, including the novelist George Meredith, encouraged Hardy to continue writing. In 1871 *Desperate Remedies* was published (though Hardy himself had to contribute towards the expenses of publication). Despite an unenthusiastic reception he persevered with a novel based, for the first time, on Dorset and its people; *Under the Greenwood Tree* (1872), though not a great commercial success, pleased the critics and led the distinguished

Cornhill magazine to commission a novel from him. He first had to finish *A Pair of Blue Eyes,* which was promised for another publisher, but in 1874 serial publication of his best novel to date, *Far from the Madding Crowd,* began in the *Cornhill* and Hardy met with his first real critical and popular success. Now, as a result, he was able finally to give up the profession of architect (though he had achieved some success, winning two architectural prizes). In the same year he married.

He was now a full-time writer, and produced a steady stream of novels, not all equally successful, but gradually increasing his reputation. *The Return of the Native* (1878), *The Mayor of Casterbridge* (1885), and *The Woodlanders* (1887) are the best of the novels before *Tess.*

The reaction of critics to Hardy's work was always mixed, but nothing prepared him for the storms which were to break out over his last two novels, *Tess of the d'Urbervilles* (1891) and *Jude the Obscure* (1895). Though some critics acknowledged their power, many were offended by the way they challenged many accepted Victorian assumptions about society, sexual morality, and religion. Though the scandal meant that sales were very good, Hardy was upset by the reaction, and declared that he was tired of 'being shot at'. From that time he gave up writing novels, and turned again to his first love, poetry.

He had written verse throughout his life, but the next thirty years saw an astonishing creativity. He produced a mass of poetry, as well as the long verse-drama about the Napoleonic wars, *The Dynasts.* Gradually he has come to be regarded as one of the finest poets of this century, and any student who wishes to get a full picture of Hardy's genius should at least sample his verse.

When Hardy died in 1928 he had become a rich man, regarded universally as one of the greatest literary figures of his age, honoured by degrees from several universities and by the award of the Order of Merit. His body was buried in Westminster Abbey alongside the remains of many of Britain's greatest writers, though his heart, appropriately, lies in the churchyard at Stinsford, in the parish where he was born.

This is only an outline of the story of the shy, diffident country boy who came to be received and honoured by the most important people in the land. If we are to understand him fully, and see what is useful for the understanding of his work, then we need to go beyond the external facts.

Dorset and social class

Hardy was the first English novelist to write about the countryside and its inhabitants in a serious fashion, and obviously he drew constantly on the inspiration offered him by the people of the county in which he was born and spent most of his life. At the time of Hardy's birth Dorset was one of the poorest of English counties, but its isolation from the outside world meant that local customs and traditions were preserved unusually strongly there. In Hardy's youth things began to change. The coming of the railway in 1847 brought town and country closer together, and at the same time, for a number of different reasons, there was a growing tendency for people to leave the land for life in the cities, or else to give up the old settled way of life for a seasonal migration from job to job. Inevitably this meant that the conditions under which traditions, customs and stories passed from generation to generation no longer existed. Hardy writes about this with regret in *Tess*, Chapter 51.

Hardy's attitude to these changes was not a simple one. For while he deeply regretted the loss of the sense of belonging to a particular place, and (as we see in *Tess*) felt little sympathy for the replacement of men by machines, at the same time he was realistic enough to be genuinely glad that the conditions of great poverty which he knew in his youth were becoming rarer.

Hardy came from the peasant class himself, and it is often claimed that he writes as a spokesman for their values against those of the middle class. But though he remained a socialist throughout his life, and wrote his first, unpublished novel as a 'radical' work, this view is far too simple. He certainly does often seem to prefer the instinctive, natural values of the peasant class to the narrow-minded preoccupations of the middle classes. (Dairyman Crick's household in *Tess,* Chapter 20 is presented as an ideal.) But at the same time he was impatient with any over-romantic view of the class as a whole, and, as *Tess* shows, felt that the old way of life had lost its vigour and had to die. Moreover, in his own life he had made great efforts to educate himself precisely in order to escape from the class into which he was born. He could not be expected to deny the value of what he had spent his life achieving. But, sadly, he felt that all his learning had taught him was the truth that the universe was a hostile place, and sometimes seemed to wish that it were possible to return to a state of ignorance. So, though he could not deny absolutely that it was right to aspire to move away from peasant ignorance, he was bitterly aware of the disillusion which could result. In one way or another this dilemma is dramatised in most of his major novels. Hardy had a strong emotional attachment to a way of life and set of values from which he had moved away in his own intellectual life.

Religion

As a boy Hardy was firmly brought up as a Christian; he read the Bible and knew the words of the church services by heart. At various times he seriously considered the possibility of becoming a minister of the Church. But in his late twenties this faith disappeared. A belief that the world was governed by the careless operation of chance is reflected in all his novels.

In the Victorian period this loss of faith was an experience shared by many people. The religious enthusiasm which characterised the earlier part of the century had often degenerated into a bigoted and unappealing closed-mindedness. The publication of Darwin's *Origin of Species* (1859) which seemed to undermine the literal truth of the biblical account of the creation is often taken as one of the important events which helped to crystallise the crisis of faith. Certainly the consequence of the controversy which followed, together with many other factors, was that many people adopted a position of 'agnosticism' (a word which means literally 'not knowing').

Hardy was influenced by his reading of Darwin, of Huxley's *Essays*, which defended Darwin's work, as well as philosophy and theology of all sorts. He was also influenced strongly by two friends; Horace Moule, who introduced him to the London literary world, as well as to liberal theology, and then, after Moule's suicide (an event which profoundly disturbed Hardy), by Leslie Stephen, who first met Hardy when editing the *Cornhill*, and then became the strongest single influence on the formulation of his philosophy. More direct, though, than these influences was Hardy's own experience of human suffering and what he thought to be the world's unfairness, which he could not reconcile with Christian teaching.

Though Hardy rejected Christianity intellectually, he was nevertheless throughout his life influenced by, and attracted to, his childhood faith. He attended church sporadically, indeed used the adjective 'churchy' to describe himself; the amount of Christianity he absorbed in his youth is demonstrated by the large number of quotations from the Bible in his works. So, again, we have in Hardy a tension between what his intellect told him – that the Christian faith was untenable – and his emotional desire to believe in it.

Loves and marriage

Nearly all Hardy's novels are concerned with love and marriage. In them it seems as if he thought that the feelings of falling in love were to be celebrated, but held out little hope for the success of marriage, especially between people of different social classes. Critics have not been slow to find an explanation for this attitude in the fact that Hardy's own first marriage was not a success.

His first wife, Emma Gifford, whom he met while carrying out an architectural commission at St Juliot in Cornwall, was of the middle class, the daughter of a solicitor. Hardy was attracted by her lively personality, her interest in poetry, and by her confidence in him as a writer. When *Under the Greenwood Tree* was rejected by one publisher and Hardy almost gave up writing, it was her encouragement which persuaded him to continue. Later, however, fundamental differences of temperament and religious belief spoilt their relationship.

When Emma died in 1912, Hardy immediately wrote a large number of his best poems, which looked back to the time when they had first met, married, and been happy. In the same way, we learn about his feelings for other girls he had loved, village girls, or the series of relationships with three cousins, Rebecca, Maria and Tryphena Sparks (he was engaged to the last of them), in poetry written long after the event. It seems as if, for Hardy, relationships with women lived most vividly in his mind when they were irrevocably over. He believed passionately in the spiritual power of love, but he also believed that such love could not survive the day-to-day nearness of marriage. The feeling which emerges again and again from his love poetry is a wondering about what might have been, the unfulfilled possibility.

Hardy's feelings for women and love, like his attitude to the Christian faith or the peasant community, are intricate, complex, even self-contradictory ones. When talking about Hardy's novels it is unwise to talk in general terms about 'Hardy's view of . . .' because he seldom held simple feelings, even if he did often express dogmatic views. Out of the unresolved contradictions in his personality much of the richness of his work comes. He does not present a neatly ordered view of the world, and that is his strength as a writer.

Literary background

When Hardy was a young man Dickens (1812–70) and Thackeray (1811–63) were the most eminent living novelists, but as their subject was town life, they had little direct influence on his best writing. George Eliot (1819–80) did take provincial life as her subject, and her ideas had much in common with Hardy's. Indeed, when *Far from the Madding Crowd* was first published anonymously, some critics thought it might be George Eliot's work. She was more interested in the middle class than the peasantry, and was perhaps a more consciously 'intellectual' writer than Hardy, but he had great respect for her, though he judged her, rather arrogantly, 'no story-teller'. If Hardy owed any direct debt to other novelists it was to the authors he read in his earliest years – to Sir Walter Scott (1771–1832), Alexandre Dumas (1802–70), some eighteenth-century novelists, and the writers of popular historical novels. Their influence often seems unfortunate, especially in his weakness for melodramatic plots and a rather laboured style.

Hardy seems to have been more influenced by poets and poetry. In his youth he was familiar with the traditional ballads of the countryside, and their simple stories of misfortune in love, seduction and desertion, and the melancholy which is their characteristic mood often underlies his apparently complicated constructions. In his later reading he came to know Shakespeare (1564–1616) and Milton (1608–74) well, and was particularly close to the Romantic poets of the early nineteenth century. Wordsworth's (1770–1850) fidelity to nature and sense of the dignity of rural characters, and Shelley's (1792–1822) rhapsodic poetry and free-thinking ideas were a constant source of inspiration. He had a great admiration for Swinburne (1837–1909), among his contemporaries, partly at least because the poet, like Hardy, had shocked Victorian society with his anti-Christian ideas.

A note on the text

In the nineteenth century it was usual for novelists to publish their work first as a serial in one of the many magazines available, before bringing it out in book form. This obviously affected the way novelists designed their work, for if the serial was to be a success, every episode had to have something in it which would arouse and keep the interest of the readers, and so persuade them to buy the next issue. Another factor affecting novelists was that the editors of the magazines were very careful not to publish anything which they thought would offend their family readership. Hardy had problems with editorial censorship throughout his career, but these difficulties were especially marked in the case of *Tess*.

He began the novel in 1888 for Tillotson and Sons, but when he sent them the first half they rejected it as unsuitable for their family readership. Further refusals from *Murray's* and *Macmillan's* magazines followed. Hardy then decided to produce a version which would be acceptable, omitting, as he says in the 'Explanatory Note', two scenes, and making other smaller changes; this version the *Graphic* accepted. In between the rejections and the final acceptance many changes were made apart from those which the taste of editors and public seemed to force Hardy to make. During this period of revision and alteration Hardy stressed Tess's d'Urberville ancestry, and gave Alec the name d'Urberville. Even after the novel was published in book form in 1891, Hardy continued to revise small details for the editions of 1892, 1895 and 1912. It is possible to study these changes in detail, since Hardy's original manuscript survives, and it shows us that Hardy took immense trouble in preparing and revising his work. Whatever we may think of the finished product, it is the result of careful thought and painstaking attention to detail. (See Part 5, Suggestions for further reading.)

Part 2

Summaries
of TESS OF THE D'URBERVILLES

A general summary

As the title implies, *Tess of the d'Urbervilles* is basically the story of a country girl, Tess Durbeyfield. It is divided into seven 'phases' all but one of which have titles directly to do with the various stages of her life. In Phase the First, 'The Maiden', we are introduced to the innocent sixteen-year-old girl, living in the village of Marlott, her home a small house crowded with six children, and ruled by a mother and father careless of their responsibilities. We learn at the beginning of the story that in past ages the Durbeyfield family, under the name d'Urberville, had been one of the most important in the area. Though this is a matter for pride and vain boasting on the part of her father, for Tess the knowledge is disastrous. The first misfortune it brings is to suggest to her parents that, when the family fortunes suffer after the death of their horse in an accident, Tess should seek out a lady named d'Urberville, and claim help from her on the grounds of their relationship. In fact there is no kinship, the name has only been assumed, and the consequence is that Tess is brought into contact with the lady's son, Alec, a lustful, unprincipled and cruel young man, who thrusts his attentions on her.

When Phase the Second, 'Maiden no more', opens, Tess is returning from Trantridge, Alec's home, expecting his child. Though, finally, Tess plucks up sufficient courage to face people, after the death of the child she decides it would be better for her to look for a job elsewhere.

Phase the Third, 'The Rally', presents us with the only really happy time in Tess's life. Working as a dairymaid at Talbothays she meets Angel Clare (who had briefly entered her life at the beginning of the book). He is a clergyman's son, a gentleman, who has taken the unlikely course of working on a farm because, denied a university education as he did not share the Christian faith of his family, he plans to learn about farming through practical experience. Gradually he falls in love with Tess, and she with him.

As this love develops further towards an apparently inevitable marriage in Phase the Fourth, 'The Consequence', Tess struggles with her conscience, feeling the pressure of society's view that what had happened to her was 'sinful', ashamed of deceiving Angel by not telling him, but fearful of the consequences if he knew. Chance prevents a letter in which she tells the story being read by Angel, and so it is not until their wedding-night, after Angel has himself confessed youthful mis-behaviour, that her secret emerges.

Then begins a new period of suffering for Tess. Phase the Fifth is aptly called 'The Woman Pays'. In it Angel leaves his wife, unable to bring himself to live with the real woman who has replaced the idealised picture he had of her in his mind. He decides to emigrate to Brazil, where one day Tess might join him. He leaves her money, but it gradually disappears, partly because Tess gives most of it to her family, from whom she conceals the truth of what has happened. She has, therefore, to work, and finally ends up toiling in the harsh winter weather at Flintcomb-Ash farm. Eventually, hearing nothing of Angel, she buries her pride and sets off to see his family; unfortunately she overhears harsh comments made about her by Angel's brothers, and never meets his parents. Making her despondent way back she encounters the unlikely sight of her former lover, Alec d'Urberville, preaching as a recent convert to Christianity.

In Phase the Sixth, 'The Convert', Alec's temporary faith wears off as he resumes his attentions to Tess. He presses his case insidiously by offering to take care of her family. Soon they have need of help, for after the death of Tess's father, the Durbeyfields (Tess has now returned home) are forced to leave their house, and can find no lodging. In Phase the Seventh Angel returns from Brazil having suffered physically and repented of his action in leaving his wife. He now finds Tess has, though unwillingly, gone back to Alec, who fulfilled his promise to provide for her family. In bitter anger Tess murders Alec, and for a brief week finds happiness with Angel, until the police surround her at Stonehenge and take her away to execution.

Detailed summaries

The glossary which follows the summary of each chapter is intended to give information about Hardy's quotations and other references, and to explain *some* of the less familiar words he uses. It cannot, obviously, be complete, and students are advised to consult a good dictionary (one of the Oxford dictionaries, for example) for individual words, and the notes to the New Wessex Edition for more extended information on other matters.

The comments which follow the annotations aim to bring various different kinds of points to the student's attention as he is reading through the book. Again, they make no claim to completeness of any kind, but are intended to be suggestive and helpful in close reading of the text, and also to prepare for the more extended discussion in the fourth section.

Phase the First · The Maiden · Chapter 1

As Jack Durbeyfield is walking drunkenly home, he is surprised when
Parson Tringham greets him as 'Sir John'. The parson explains that he
has discovered that 'Durbeyfield' is a corruption of the name
'd'Urberville', and that Jack's ancestors were once important people in
the area. Jack is gratified by the news, and orders a boy to fetch him a
carriage appropriate to his station, and to run home to prepare his wife
for his return. The chapter closes with the sound of a club-walking in
which Jack's daughter, Tess, is involved.

COMMENTARY: Hardy strongly emphasises the theme of Tess's ancestry
by choosing to open the book with this incident.

Notice the way the scene is drawn in a very detached way; it is built up
entirely by description. Hardy begins many chapters in this way.

In this chapter many small details prepare the reader for what is to
come later. One example is the way Parson Tringham notices a
resemblance between Jack and his ancestors, as Angel Clare is going to
notice the similarity of Tess to portraits of her forbears in Chapter 34.

NOTES AND GLOSSARY:

haggler:	a travelling dealer
d'Urbervilles:	the name and history suggested by the real Dorset family of Turbeville
Battle Abbey Roll:	records kept at the abbey founded at the place of the battle of Hastings (1066) when the Normans, under William, successfully invaded England and defeated Harold
Pipe Roll:	early records of the Kings of England
King Stephen:	reigned from 1135 to 1154
King John:	reigned from 1199 to 1216
King Edward II:	reigned from 1307 to 1327
Oliver Cromwell:	Lord Protector from 1649 to 1658
Charles II:	reigned from 1660 to 1685
wold:	*(dialect)* old
mendacious:	untruthful
'how are the mighty fallen':	from the Bible, 2 Samuel 1:19
skillentons:	*(dialect)* skeletons
shilling:	five new pence (then worth a great deal more)
lamb's fry:	sheep's organs
black-pot:	black pudding, a sausage made from pig's blood
chitterlings:	pig's intestine (all three the food of poor people)
club-walking:	annual celebration of a village mutual benefit society
vamp:	*(dialect)* trudge

Chapter 2

A description of the Vale of Blackmoor and the village of Marlott leads to the presentation of the club-walking. Tess is embarrassed when the other girls catch sight of her drunken father being driven home. As the dance goes on three men, Angel Clare and his brothers, stop to watch. While the others continue on their way Angel stays to join in, though as chance has it he does not dance with Tess, only becoming aware of her as he leaves.

COMMENTARY: We learn both about the present and the past of the place, and of the club-walking festivities in a way which is very typical of Hardy. The story of the killing of a beautiful white hart foreshadows the tragedy which is about to begin.

The class prejudice which is to be a constant theme in the book is introduced by the contempt of the Clare brothers for the girls at the club-walking.

NOTES AND GLOSSARY:

calcareous:	containing limestone
plashed:	interwoven
King Henry III:	1216–72
Cerealia:	Roman feast in honour of Ceres, goddess of corn and fruitfulness
Old Style:	in 1752 the calendar was changed and called the New Style
'I have no pleasure in them':	from the Bible, Ecclesiastes 12:1
factotum:	one who does everything
market-nitch:	*(dialect)* fill of drink on market-day
uncribbed, uncabined:	echo of Shakespeare's *Macbeth* III. 4, meaning 'free, unconstrained'
Angel:	the unusual name was suggested to Hardy by a memorial in Stinsford parish church
hoyden:	contemptuous term for a young girl
'A Counterblast to Agnosticism':	a fictional title, but typical of Victorian religious controversy
clipsing and colling:	*(dialect)* hugging and embracing

Chapter 3

Tess returns home to find her mother busily occupied, and her father still out drinking. Joan refuses Tess's offer to go and fetch him, wishing herself to escape from the house for a time. Her father (who has heart disease) has to set out early the next day, so Tess is concerned when neither return. She first sends her young brother Abraham, then goes herself to bring them back.

COMMENTARY: The contrast between the festival atmosphere and the dreary home is established through Tess's eyes, though at other points in the chapter we hear Hardy speaking in his own voice, offering comments on the unfortunate plight of the children of such parents, or expressing Mrs Durbeyfield's thoughts in language she could never use. He seems to be using the contrast between Mrs Durbeyfield's heavy use of dialect words and his own rather elevated style to make a comment on her limitations.

NOTES AND GLOSSARY:

gallopade:	lively dance-tune
diment:	*(dialect)* diamond
Cubit's:	Joan's version of 'Cupid's' (the Roman god of love)
fess:	*(dialect)* pleased
National School:	a school founded by the Church for the benefit of the poor (established before the State took over the provision of education for everyone)
mommet:	*(dialect)* scarecrow
thik:	*(dialect)* that
larry:	*(dialect)* confusion
Oliver Grumble:	Joan's uneducated version of Oliver Cromwell
Saint Charles:	a real confusion; Charles II, who is meant, was anything but a saint. His father, Charles I, executed at the time of the Civil War, is sometimes held to be a religious martyr
plim:	*(dialect)* swell
vlee:	*(dialect)* one-horse carriage
mampus:	*(dialect)* crowd
volk:	*(dialect)* folk
shadder:	*(dialect)* shadow
mid:	*(dialect)* might
Revised Code:	(1862) a scheme to raise educational standards
Jacobean:	of the time of James I (reigned 1603–25)
'Nature's Holy plan':	from Wordsworth's, 'Lines written in early spring'
bain't:	be not

Chapter 4

We return in time to Mrs Durbeyfield's arrival at Rolliver's, where she tells her husband of her scheme to get Tess to make the acquaintance of the rich Mrs d'Urberville (whom she believes to be a relation) and perhaps thereby to secure herself a husband. Abraham arrives, then

Tess, and the family return home. The next morning Jack has not recovered, so Tess and Abraham set out for market. On the way Abraham tells of the scheme he has overheard. They both fall asleep, to be awoken when the horse is killed by the shafts of the oncoming night-mail. Tess blames herself for losing the family's means of livelihood.

COMMENTARY: A number of hints of what is to come are contained in the chapter; for example, mention of possible pregnancy, and the fact that Tess regards herself as a 'murderess' – which she is actually to become.

Perhaps Hardy tries too hard to prepare the reader for the ultimate tragedy of the novel in the discussion between Abraham and Tess about a 'blighted world', which is surely too sophisticated for a nine-year-old boy.

NOTES AND GLOSSARY:

cwoffer:	*(dialect)* coffer, chest
Solomon's temple:	see the Bible, 1 Kings 7:15–22
gaffer:	official
projick:	project
kin to a coach:	related to a family that can afford a coach
sumple:	*(dialect)* supple
get green malt in floor:	become pregnant
eastings or genuflections:	turnings to the east and bending the knee
nater:	nature
audition:	being listened to
stubbard-tree:	early apple tree
knacker:	horse-slaughterer

Chapter 5

The Durbeyfield family's fortunes decline, and Tess is finally persuaded to visit Mrs d'Urberville to get help. The history of the d'Urbervilles is given – they made a fortune in manufacturing and simply chose the name at random. When Tess arrives at the new-looking house, 'The Slopes', she is met by the son, Alec, who explains that his mother is ill. He gives her strawberries, roses and food, but does not take her into the house. He is attracted to her, and 'thus the thing began'; as Tess sets off home Hardy reflects on the pity that Angel Clare was not the one there are the vital time.

COMMENTARY: The d'Urberville house is appropriately new for a family not rooted in the country, and is clearly distinguished from the surrounding ageless countryside (see also Chapter 9).

Remark Tess's reluctance to seek help from 'relatives'; this looks forward to her slowness in approaching Angel's family in the latter stages of the book.

Something of Hardy's philosophy is contained in the last paragraph, which repays close attention.

NOTES AND GLOSSARY:

good-now:	*(dialect)* equivalent to 'I guess' or 'you know'
Malthusian:	Thomas Malthus (1766–1834) pointed to the way population increases faster than the means of providing for it
Druidical misletoe:	the pre-Christian priests, the Druids, held misletoe to be especially sacred
pollarded:	had branches lopped off
Chapels-of-Ease:	churches built for the convenience of those who lived away from the parish church
Coz:	literally 'cousin'; colloquially a term of familiarity
crumby:	*(slang)* appealing

Chapter 6

Tess arrives home after staying the night with a friend, to find that a letter has been delivered by Alec d'Urberville asking her to look after the poultry-farm. The family are pleased at the prospect, and when Tess is unable to find other work she finally agrees to go.

COMMENTARY: Much of Tess's story is to be dictated by her success or lack of it in finding work, a motif which is emphasised in this chapter.

To her family the adventure is as much a social one – being 'made a lady' – as a monetary one; social advancement, however, does not matter to Tess herself.

NOTES AND GLOSSARY:

dolorifuge:	a chaser away of sorrow
fairlings:	*(dialect)* things brought at a fair
spring-cart:	a cart with spring suspension

Chapter 7

Tess is dressed up by her mother to set out for her job. Alec arrives in a smart carriage and persuades Tess to go with him, leaving her luggage for the spring-cart. Though Tess is only interested in earning money, her family expect a marriage; but after she has gone the children cry, and Mrs Durbeyfield has doubts.

COMMENTARY: Notice that Tess is dressed in the same clothes she had worn when Angel Clare first noticed her; this is one of the many ways Hardy links the two men in Tess's life together.

The Durbeyfield family's very casual moral attitudes are made clear, both by Jack's willingness to sell the title of which at other times he is proud, and, even more significantly, by Joan's belief that even if Tess is wronged by Alec he will marry her and make things right.

NOTES AND GLOSSARY:

dand:	*(dialect)* dandy; smart dresser
acclivity:	upward slope
lammicken:	*(dialect)* clumsy
gig or dog-cart:	kinds of carriage
buck:	smart young man
choice over her:	attracted by her

Chapter 8

On the journey Alec frightens Tess by the speed at which he drives, and unconsciously she holds on to him. He demands a kiss as the price for going slower. Tess agrees, but her reluctance angers him, and Tess lets her hat fall off so that he has to stop. She dismounts and refuses to get back, preferring to walk alongside the carriage until they arrive at The Slopes.

COMMENTARY: Hardy achieves the impression of the speed of the carriage not by short, sharp words, but by the exactness of his description.

   We learn a lot about Alec in this chapter, especially the way he delights in 'mastery', both of his horse and of Tess. Notice also the sneer 'you're mighty sensitive for a cottage girl' – a class-conscious remark, like that of Angel's brothers, assuming that peasant girls have no moral scruples.

NOTES AND GLOSSARY:
holmberry: holly berry

Chapter 9

Tess begins her duties, which involve both looking after the poultry and whistling tunes to the blind Mrs d'Urberville's pet bullfinches. Alec teaches Tess to whistle, but is not over attentive to her, and she accepts his presence.

COMMENTARY: The image of fowl living in what were once villager's houses is a powerful one for the impermanence of rural communities; it foreshadows the way the Durbeyfield family have to leave their house when Jack dies (Chapter 50).

It is only here that we hear of the relationship between Mrs d'Urberville and her son, her feeling of bitter love. (Alec later claims the death of his mother influenced him deeply.)

NOTES AND GLOSSARY:

copyholders: men who held land according to conditions laid down in the 'copy' of the manorial roll. Their tenure often lasted for a certain number of generations only

severally: one at a time

Confirmation: the ceremony by which children are made full members of the Church

sitting like *Im*-patience on a monument: a version of the line 'she sat like Patience on a monument'; Shakespeare, *Twelfth Night*, II.4

'Take, O take those lips away': first line of a song from Shakespeare, *Measure for Measure*, IV.1

out of her books: *(colloquial)* out of favour

freak: whim

Chapter 10

The villagers of Trantridge make a weekly expedition to Chaseborough, which Tess becomes used to joining. Once, after about two months, she sets out later than the others, and has to search for them to accompany her home. They are at a dance, which goes on late. Alec appears and offers to take her home, but she refuses. When they finally set off, some rather drunk, an argument breaks out, and Tess, wanting to escape, agrees to go with Alec, who has ridden up suddenly. The villagers suspect what will happen, but continue homewards in an alcoholic haze.

COMMENTARY: There are many parallels between the description of the feelings of the characters under the influence of drink in this chapter, and the similar passage describing the scene at Rolliver's in Chapter 4. Hardy seems to be suggesting that only under the influence of alcohol can people feel contented and at one with nature.

All the classical allusions are to stories of passion, thus preparing the reader for the next chapter; but whereas Syrinx and Lotis were able to escape, Tess does not.

NOTES AND GLOSSARY:

Every village . . .: in the days before increased mobility this was true

the choice spirit: Alec d'Urberville (who is anything but 'choice')

parish relief: charity money for the poor

once independent inns: originally (as in Chapter 1) all inns brewed their own beers. A sign of decline, in Hardy's view

Pan, Syrinx: in Classical mythology the water nymph, Syrinx, was pursued by the lustful rural god, Pan. The other gods for pity turned her into a reed

Lotis, Priapus:	when Lotis, daughter of the sea-god, was pursued by the god of sexuality she was turned into a Lotus
Sileni:	plural of Silenus, the drunken companion of Bacchus, god of wine
jints:	*(dialect)* joints
nimbus:	the circle of halo around the head of a saint in pictures
Praxitelean:	Praxiteles was a famous Greek sculptor of the fourth century BC

Chapter 11

Tess and Alec ride off; in conversation he presses her to admit that she loves him, and tells her of gifts sent to her family. The horse is allowed to wander off the road home, and when Tess becomes suspicious Alec leaves her while he finds the way – difficult because of a fog. He returns and finds Tess sleeping.

COMMENTARY: This is the scene omitted in the serial version. Notice the way Hardy begins the scene with a lot of dialogue, generating tension between Alec and Tess, and ends in a more reflective, descriptive style.

Notice the way the fog creeps up – mist and fog are frequently used symbols in the novel.

NOTES AND GLOSSARY:

the ironical Tishbite: Elijah, describing Baal, the 'heathen' god (see the Bible, I Kings 18:27)

Phase the Second · Maiden No More · Chapter 12

A few weeks afterwards Tess is making her way home. Alec overtakes her, and indifferently she agrees to let him drive her. As she is walking the last part of her journey she meets a man writing biblical texts on walls, and is shamed by what she reads. She tells her mother what has happened, but the main reaction is only disappointment that she had not married Alec.

COMMENTARY: This chapter, like the novel's first, begins with a detached description of someone making a journey on foot; but the season is now autumn, in contrast to the spring described in the opening of the novel.

The writer of texts is often criticised as implausible, but Hardy seems to be using him mainly as a device to symbolise the narrow morality of latter-day Christianity, a force which prevents Tess coming to terms with herself.

The phrase '*social* salvation' suggests the possibility of Tess marrying Alec.

NOTES AND GLOSSARY:

serpent hisses:	reference to Satan, who tempted Eve in the form of a serpent
sweet birds sing:	recollection of Shakespeare, Sonnet 73, line 4
term:	statue of classical god Terminus, placed at boundaries
barked-oak twigs:	twigs stripped of their bark
teave:	*(dialect)* struggle
fend hands against:	*(dialect)* ward off
hontish:	*(dialect)* haughty

Chapter 13

After her return, though sometimes able to forget and face the world at a church service, Tess spends most of her time alone, walking at evening, and feeling a guilt for what she has done which Hardy tells us is guilt only in the eyes of society, not of nature.

COMMENTARY: In this chapter Hardy directs the reader, telling him what he is to think about the pretended piety of the church congregation, or about Tess's feelings of guilt. Perhaps he is preaching too obviously.

NOTES AND GLOSSARY:

Robert South:	(1634–1716) a famous preacher
chiming:	a church service is announced by the ringing of bells
lumber:	store of various bits and pieces
bier:	stand upon which a coffin is placed (a melancholy detail, characteristic of Hardy)
Langdon:	tunes for hymns and psalms are referred to by their composer; here, Richard Langdon (1730–1803)

Chapter 14

It is August, and among the harvesters is Tess, finally reconciled to going into the outside world. At the meal-break her child is brought to her, and she feeds it. When she returns home she finds the child is ill; she wishes it to be baptised, but her father prevents her from fetching the clergyman. With the help of her brothers and sisters, she herself baptises the baby Sorrow, just before he dies. The vicar assures her that the christening was all right, but refuses to bury the baby in consecrated ground.

COMMENTARY: The baptism of Sorrow was omitted from the serial version. Its attack on clergymen, and the bitter irony at the expense of the sacrament of baptism would have offended (as indeed it probably still does) believing Christians.

The opening of this chapter, in sharp distinction to the end of the last, is written in a very detached style (Hardy speaks of 'the eye') – it is a long time before our attention is focussed on Tess.

NOTES AND GLOSSARY:

heliolatries: forms of sun-worship

Maltese cross: four equal arms, widening towards their ends

reaping-machine: introduced in 1862

shock: small heap of corn sheaves

gold-leaf halo . . . saint: referring to paintings of saints, by Italian artists

burn: the damned are burnt in Hell

Aholah and Aholibah: biblical harlots

no salvation: according to the Christian doctrine, only those who have been received into the church by baptism can enter heaven

a phrase . . . Genesis: Rachel's son was named Ben-oni, Hebrew for 'son of my sorrow'

stopt-diapason: one of the sounds of the pipe-organ; full and flute like

---

Chapter 15

Tess thinks back over her past, and looks forward to her future. Her experiences have turned her from girl to woman. Eventually, stirred by the renewing of life in the spring, she decides to move away from Marlott to take up a job as a dairymaid at Talbothays, where no one will know of her past.

COMMENTARY: This chapter guides our view of Tess's character and illustrates her kinship with nature. All the previous events of her life are summarised in her thoughts, making a neat ending to this phase of her life.

NOTES AND GLOSSARY:

Robert Ascham: (1515–68) from his work *The Schoolmaster*

Saint Augustine: (AD 354–430) one of the early fathers of the Church. His influential *Confessions* tell of his own spiritual struggles

Jeremy Taylor: (1613–67) a divine; quotation from *Holy Dying*

Phase the Third · The Ralley · Chapter 16

Tess sets out in May, two years after her return from Trantridge, full of a natural optimism (she is still only twenty), and arrives at Talbothays at milking time.

COMMENTARY: Tess's optimism is conveyed by different means, including the general fruitfulness of the scene through which she passes.

NOTES AND GLOSSARY:

Van Asloot; Salleart: seventeenth-century Flemish painters

River of Life: seen by John (the Evangelist) in the vision recorded in the Bible, Revelation 22

she had eaten . . . knowledge: Eve's eating of the forbidden tree brought about the expulsion of man from Paradise. See the Bible, Genesis 3

'O ye Sun and Moon . . .': words from the Benedicite, sung at morning service

steading: outbuiding

barton: farmyard

milchers: cows which give milk

Olympian: the classical gods lived on Mount Olympus

Chapter 17

Tess sets to milking. When it seems that the cows are not giving their milk freely a song is called for, and then one of the dairymen is asked to play a tune on his harp. (This provokes a retelling of an old story of a fiddler pacifying a bull.) The harpist is later revealed to Tess as the man who had briefly joined the club-walking dance; that night one of the milkmaids tells her that he is Angel Clare, son of a clergyman, who is learning farming.

COMMENTARY: Even in this generally contented scene Hardy reminds us that this is a landscape 'compounded of old landscapes', and the funny story is told about a man 'a-lying in Mellstock churchyard'.

NOTES AND GLOSSARY:

pattens: wooden overshoes

pinner: *(dialect)* apron

broad-cloth: thick black material

terminatively: in conclusion

cowcumber: *(dialect)* cucumber

kex: dry stem of certain plants

nott: *(dialect)* without horns

stave: a line of music, hence a song

William Dewey: character in Hardy's *Under the Greenwood Tree*

tranter: a carrier of goods

do ye mind: *(dialect)* do you recall

leery: *(dialect)* empty, hungry

stuff: woollen material

leads:	leaden milk-pans
Low Church:	the Evangelical wing of the Anglican Church; emphasis on preaching, very plain services
High (Church):	the branch of the Anglican Church nearest to Roman Catholic, with an emphasis on ritual
wrings:	cheese presses

Chapter 18

Angel Clare's past rebellion against the Christian faith of his father, his failure therefore to go to University, and his decision to take up farming are related. A few days after her arrival he notices Tess, finding her the most attractive of the dairymaids.

COMMENTARY: Angel's comments on the church, beginning 'I shall always have the warmest affection for her' are very like Hardy's own feelings.

Hardy prepares for things to come, both directly, by telling us of Clare's affair with a woman in London, and indirectly, when Dairyman Crick's knife and fork are poised like a gallows just before Tess tells how the spirit may leave the body, thus preparing for the feelings of the scene at Stonehenge (Chapter 58).

NOTES AND GLOSSARY:

redemptive theolatry:	the Christian belief in the salvation of man by the redeeming sacrifice of Christ on the cross
thimble-riggers:	cheats
Evangelical:	emphasising the special importance of the words of the Bible in the Christian life
'Indeed opine . . .':	from Browning's *Easter Day*, stanza 8
Article Four:	the basic beliefs of the Anglican church, to which every minister has to subscribe in a Declaration, are contained in the 'Thirty-Nine Articles'. The fourth concerns belief in Christ's resurrection from the dead
'the removing . . .':	see the Bible, Epistle to the Hebrews, 12:27
Hodge:	conventional literary name for caricature of the peasant
Pascal:	(1632–62) French philosopher. 'The more intelligence a man has, the more he will recognise the distinctiveness of other people. Ordinary people do not see any differences between men.'
Miltonic . . . Cromwellian:	reference to Gray's 'Elegy in a Country Churchyard', stanza 15

road to dusty death: a quotation from Shakespeare, *Macbeth* V.5
mess: eat together
mullioned: divided by vertical stone bar

Chapter 19

Tess, hearing Angel playing his harp, finds him and talks to him about life. He is surprised, since he does not know of her experience, at the bitterness of some of her statements; she, not knowing his past, is equally surprised at a gentleman wanting to be a farmer. Tess wonders if knowing about her ancestry would make Angel favour her more, but the dairyman tells her that Clare hates old families.

COMMENTARY: Though the meeting is set in a fine June scene, Tess makes her way to Angel through rank ground (reminiscent of Sorrow's burial-place); the mist of pollen recalls the scene of the dance at Chaseborough. Thus both passion and pain are suggested here by the cross-references.

There is a great deal of delicacy in this dialogue; Hardy makes Tess's speech very convincingly that of a country girl with some education.

NOTES AND GLOSSARY:
cuckoo-spittle: secretion of insects, like froth
blights: mildew
apple-blooth: *(dialect)* apple-blossom
hobble: *(dialect)* awkward fact
Valley of Humiliation: in Bunyan's (1628–88) *Pilgrim's Progress*
man of Uz: Job, the biblical example of extreme suffering
Peter the Great: Emperor of Russia, who studied in foreign ship-yards 1697–8 before building his own navy
Abraham: in the Bible, he possessed many animals and servants
Andean: like the Andes, South American mountains
'lords and ladies': small kind of lily
Queen of Sheba: biblical character, overwhelmed by Solomon's magnificence
shine on the just . . . alike: see the Bible, Matthew 5:25
niaiseries: *(French)* foolishness
rozum: *(dialect)* man with strange ideas
in Palestine: on the medieval Crusades

Chapter 20

Tess and Angel, meeting early every morning, are trembling on the brink of love.

COMMENTARY: A short, but very rich chapter, repaying close study. The difference in Tess's state of mind is reinforced by the comparison of the atmosphere of early morning with the evening time when she had wandered solitarily (in Chapter 13).

In the comparisons of Tess to mythological figures the earlier descriptions of the Chaseborough dancers are recalled; the fog, and the moisture on Tess's eyelashes recall the scene of her rape. An idealisation of Tess is blended with the reality; Hardy is helping the reader to see Tess as Angel sees her.

NOTES AND GLOSSARY:

convenances: *(French)* artificial social customs

aborescence: the growing of trees

as if they were Adam and Eve: another reference to the biblical story of the first man and woman in Paradise

Resurrection Hour: the time when Christ rose from the dead

Magdalen: Mary Magdalen, one of the first to see the risen Christ; she was a 'fallen woman' who repented

Artemis: Greek goddess of chastity

Demeter: Greek goddess of fruitfulness

Chapter 21

One day the milk fails to turn into butter; country superstition has it that the presence of somebody in love is the cause. A tale told by the dairyman reminds Tess of her misfortunes and she goes outside, at which point the butter begins to form. At night she overhears her companions confessing their love for Angel, and saying that he is attached to Tess. She is afraid, not only because he is a gentleman, but also because she feels she cannot allow any man to marry her.

COMMENTARY: Hardy was always interested in country superstitions, and in curious stories. Notice how well he tells them (see also Chapter 17), catching exactly the way people talk.

NOTES AND GLOSSARY:

Conjuror: a person who told fortunes and provided old country remedies

cast folk's waters: told fortunes by examining urine

touchwood: fungus infested, dry wood

Holy Thursday: the day of Christ's Ascension into Heaven

ballyragging: abusing

by side and by seam: in all sorts of ways

pummy: *(dialect)* apple pulp left after juice has been extracted for cider

dog-days:	late summer; hottest time of the year
Marian:	based on a girl whom Hardy taught in Sunday School
zid:	a dialect form of 'saw'

Chapter 22

A fault in the butter is caused by the cows feeding on wild garlic. During the search to uproot it, Tess tries to divert Angel's attentions to the other girls.

COMMENTARY: The sentence 'Angel Clare had the honour of all the dairymaids in his keeping' turns out to be truer than we might think. All, not just Tess, are to have their future lives affected by him.

NOTES AND GLOSSARY:

twang:	unpleasant flavour
communistically:	not in the modern strictly political sense

Chapter 23

Two months after her arrival at Talbothays Tess, with Marian, Retty and Izz find their road to church flooded. Angel appears and carries each of them over, telling Tess that he felt most for her. The other girls accept that Tess is favoured. In conversation that night they tell Tess that a girl has been selected by Angel's family for him to marry.

COMMENTARY: Notice the characteristic image of insects trapped in the girls' skirts. The passion of love is here called '*cruel* Nature's Law' – this seems to modify our attitude to earlier statements about Tess's affair with Alec not being contrary to Nature.

NOTES AND GLOSSARY:

'That-it-may-please-Thees':	a repeated prayer from the Litany, part of morning service
un-Sabbatarian:	it was customary to wear one's best clothes on Sunday (the Sabbath)
thistle-spud:	a tool for uprooting thistles
sermons in stones:	phrase from Shakespeare, *As You Like It* II.1
'a time to embrace':	from the Bible, Ecclesiastes 3:5
paltered:	became evasive
three Leahs to get one Rachel:	Jacob first married Leah, and only then was allowed to work to earn Rachel as his wife (see the Bible, Genesis 29)
thorny crown:	recalling the crown of thorns placed on the head of Christ before his crucifixion.

Chapter 24

In the heat of late summer Tess and Angel are milking in the fields. He is overcome by feeling and embraces Tess, protesting his love. She cries.

COMMENTARY: The oppressive season is linked with the hearts oppressed by passion.

Tess's lips are noticed by Angel as being not perfect, which gives them their humanity. It is ironic that later her imperfection sickens him.

Hardy writes in a very full and ample style at the end of the chapter, giving a firm ending to the phase of the story when Tess seems to have escaped from her past. The section ends with an incident – crying at a kiss – which seems to echo Tess's earlier seduction by Alec while emphasising the difference.

NOTES AND GLOSSARY:

Thermidorean: very hot; Thermidor was the month in the French Revolutionary calendar beginning 19 July
diurnal roll: the daily turning of the earth
cameo: relief carving in stone (often white on brown)
Elizabethan simile: a very common comparison in Elizabethan poetry
aura: *(Latin)* breath, breeze

Phase the Fourth · The Consequence · Chapter 25

This is a chapter devoted to Angel; first to his thoughts about his responsibility to Tess, then to the visit home where we see him in a family context and contrast his experience and beliefs with the views of his father and brothers.

COMMENTARY: A distinction is made throughout this chapter between the spontaneous naturalness of life as Angel has experienced it at Talbothays and his family's obsession with religion and its laws. A distinction is, however, made between Angel's father, with his sincerity and kindliness, and his less sympathetic brothers. This chapter gives the reader an idea of the habits and feelings which make possible Angel's future actions.

NOTES AND GLOSSARY:

noctambulist: walker at night
Walt Whitman: (1819–92) American poet. These lines are from 'Crossing the Brooklyn Ferry'
the creeper blushed: Hardy probably has in mind a clinging plant of reddish colour such as Virginia creeper
pachydermatous: thick-skinned

heterodoxy: unconventional beliefs

First Cause: philosophical term for that which sets the universe in motion

'pleasure girdled about with pain': from Swinburne's *Atalanta in Calydon*

mead: alcoholic drink made from honey

Antinomianism: a belief, favoured by evangelical Christians, that faith in Jesus Christ is above the moral law

court-patched: society ladies of an earlier period wore small black patches on their faces as an adornment

Wycliff, Huss, Luther, Calvin: initiators, from the fourteenth to the sixteenth centuries, of the Protestant Reformation

Christiad, Pauliad: epics on the lives of Christ and St Paul (word formation derived from *Iliad*, Homer's epic poem)

determinism: belief that the way one lives does not affect salvation or damnation in the next life, which is already known to God

Schopenhauer, Leopardi: early nineteenth-century German and Italian pessimistic philosophers

Canons: laws of the Church

Rubric: instruction for the carrying out of services

geocentric: the old belief that the earth was at the centre of the universe, hell below and heaven above

hall-marked: precious metals are stamped with a mark to guarantee their purity

Corregio: (1494–1534) Italian painter

Velasquez: (1599–1660) Spanish painter

Diocesan Synod: the assembly of clergymen

Visitation: inspection of a diocese by its bishop

dapes inemptae: *(Latin)* unbought banquet (from Vergil)

delirium tremens: literally 'trembling madness'; suffered by heavy drinkers

Chapter 26

Angel discusses with his parents the possibility of his marrying Tess. Though they are worried about the difference in social class between him and her, and advance the cause of Mercy Chant, they eventually agree to meet Tess. As Angel makes his way back to Talbothays his father tells of Alec d'Urberville having insulted him while he was preaching a sermon.

COMMENTARY: The re-entry of Alec not only reminds the reader of his past, but prepares us for the future. We also hear, in passing, of the legend of the d'Urberville coach.

Angel's views on social class, and on the possible future erosion of class distinction are very close to Hardy's own.

NOTES AND GLOSSARY:

vestal: Roman virgin who tended the temple of Vesta
epiderm: outer skin
Christologist: student of the theology of Christ's life
Calvinistic: following the teachings of Calvin; strict
'exclaim against ... succession: Shakespeare, *Hamlet* II:2
'thou fool ...': from the Bible, Luke 12:20
'being reviled ...': from the Bible, I Corinthians 4: 12–14

Chapter 27

Angel returns and meets Tess as she is getting up for the afternoon skimming. He asks her to marry him, but she refuses, and does so even more firmly after he recounts his father's experience with Alec.

COMMENTARY: The contrast between this chapter and the two which precede it accounts for a great deal of its effectiveness.

Human and animal life seem to be mixed together by the comparison of sleeping men to pigs, and then the numerous animal comparisons used in descriptions of Tess. It is an idyllic, drowsy picture, but in the first half the image of Eve (and the mention of Tess's 'snake-like mouth' – Eve was tempted by the Devil in the form of a snake), and the way Tess 'flinches' under the weight of Angel's love, prepare us for her response to his proposal, and hint at the potential tragedy of their love.

NOTES AND GLOSSARY:

fibrils: small threads
Eve at her second waking: presumably after her first sleep; another reference to the Genesis story
Tractarian: High Church movement, whose opinions were put forward in *Tracts for the Times*
Pantheistic: seeing God in all things
'Leave ... days': from Tennyson's (1809–92) *In Memoriam*

Chapter 28

Tess refuses a further proposal from Angel, but promises to give her reasons the following Sunday. She agonises over her decision, but thinks she will finally agree to accept him.

COMMENTARY: The presentation of countryfolk as more inclined than ambitious town-dwellers to accept passion for itself is not really true, for example, of Joan Durbeyfield's attitude.

The evening when Tess is in a state of distress is presented with harsh images; the sun is like a forge, the moon is monstrous. The distorted pollard willows, an example of what man can do to nature, are appropriate to Tess, whose nature is distorted by what society expects.

NOTES AND GLOSSARY:

trowing:	an old word, meaning 'believing, being aware'
'sigh gratis':	echo of *Hamlet* II. 2, meaning sigh without hope of reward
carking:	Hardy seems to have used this word in his own sense, perhaps 'worrying'
love satire:	Angel does not believe Tess has had 'experiences', therefore makes fun of her
convolvulus:	a plant which grows by twining itself round others

Chapter 29

On the Sunday morning Dairyman Crick continues the story of Jack Dollop, much to Tess's confusion. She refuses Angel again, though confessing that she loves him. One day the milking finishes so late that the milk has to be driven direct to the station. Angel offers to go, Tess agrees to accompany him.

NOTES AND GLOSSARY:

cust:	cursed
scram:	*(dialect)* weak, feeble

Chapter 30

On the journey back from the station Tess tries to tell Angel of her past, but his interruptions and her own fear make her pretend that it was only fear lest he should despise her ancient ancestry which held her back. She finally agrees to marry him.

COMMENTARY: At this turning point in Tess's life many earlier incidents are recalled. Angel himself remembers that the has seen Tess before; the reference to the celestial stars recalls the conversation between Abraham and Tess (Chapter 4); where Alec drove fast, Angel drives slowly, and is careful of her comfort.

NOTES AND GLOSSARY:

Caroline:	of the time of Charles I and II
centurions:	officers in the Roman army (Tess is unhistorical)
lucubrations:	meditations (especially at night)

Chapter 31

Tess's mother in a letter advises her against telling her past to Angel. He presses Tess to settle the day of their marriage, and their betrothal becomes public when they are surprised by the dairyman and the girls. They tell Tess that they are not jealous, but she is conscious of their purity and resolves to tell Angel her past.

COMMENTARY: This scene characterises the love of Angel and Tess effectively. Amongst much that is attractive we are made to recognise the excess, the danger of over-idealisation.

Yet again in a scene of passion we find moisture resting on Tess's eyelashes.

NOTES AND GLOSSARY:

J:	old form of I, indicating with the random use of capital letters, Joan's lack of education
Byronic:	Byron (1788–1824) both in his life and poetry celebrated sensuality
Shelleyan:	Shelley (1792–1822) presented a more spiritual enthusiasm in his poetry
champaign:	open country
photosphere:	luminous surround of a star
true and honest ... good report:	see the Bible, Philippians 4:8
springe:	trap
dogs:	metal supports for burning wood
baily:	bailiff; farm manager

Chapter 32

Hesitations about fixing the wedding-day are ended when Angel points out that milkmaids will not be needed during the winter. The end of December is named as the day, a dress is bought by Angel, and it is arranged that they will go to a house which once belonged to the d'Urberville family.

COMMENTARY: The image of the brief glory of the gnats is one of many taken from nature which emphasises the transitoriness of things. Two elements of character are brought out: Tess's passive fatalism, and Angel's tinge of recklessness.

NOTES AND GLOSSARY:

bolting:	sifting flour
banns, licence:	before a church wedding, notice must be given by reading out the names at three weekly services, unless a special licence is obtained

'that never . . . done amiss': in an old ballad a dress which changed colour if an unchaste woman wore it was brought to the court of King Arthur, the legendary British king. When given to Queen Guinevere it changed colour because of her adultery with the knight Lancelot

Chapter 33

Two incidents disturb Tess: while out shopping Angel strikes down a Trantridge man who recognises Tess and casts doubt on her virtue; at night Angel has a violent dream about the incident. Tess therefore decides to confess her past in a letter she pushes under Angel's door. She discovers on the day of the wedding that it had gone under the carpet, and had never been read. The wedding goes ahead, Tess is ecstatically happy, but as they set off together from the dairy a cock crows, an omen of disaster.

COMMENTARY: Notice how in this chapter, though it concerns Angel and Tess, Hardy concentrates mainly on Tess's feelings. The way Hardy piles misfortune, ill omens (the d'Urbeville coach, the cock), and grotesque details like the repellent coachman, one on top of the other is thought by some critics to be excessive.

NOTES AND GLOSSARY:
negatived . . . forthwith: that is, denied that she was a virgin
drachm: very small weight
blower: material fixed to increase the draught
gieing a rattling good randy: *(dialect)* giving a boisterous party
temerarious: rash
close carriage: carriage having a roof
post-chaise travelling: until the coming of the railway long distances were travelled in a coach with frequent changes of horses
felloes: wheel-rims
partie carrée: *(French)* party of four
modest peal of three notes: the normal 'peal' of church bells is six or eight bells, each striking a separate note
angel . . . sun: see the Bible, Revelation 19:17
Friar Lawrence: in *Romeo and Juliet*, Shakespeare's tragedy of young lovers

Chapter 34

Tess and Angel arrive at Wellbridge, where Tess is frightened by two pictures of her ancestors hanging on the wall which resemble her. (See notes to Chapter 1.) While they wait for their luggage some jewels are delivered from Angel's father, heirlooms to be the property of Angel's wife during her lifetime. Their luggage finally arrives, having been delayed by the misfortunes of the three milkmaids in their despair at Angel's leaving. Eventually Angel confesses his early debauchery, and she tells the story of her past.

COMMENTARY: This scene is a masterpiece of dramatic construction. The changes of mood and the steady building of tension by alternation of dialogue and description which lead to the moment of Tess's foolishly confident confession are handled with great sureness.

NOTES AND GLOSSARY:

crush:	social gathering
gallied:	*(dialect)* scared
mops and brooms . . . 'em:	presumably means senseless as brushes from over-drinking
withy-bed:	willow plantation
trencher-woman:	eater
traps:	personal belongings
night-rail:	*(dialect)* wrapper, dressing gown
Aldebaran, Sirius:	bright stars
plenary inspiration:	belief in literal truth of the Bible, because it is the Word of God
words of Paul:	see the Bible, I Timothy 6:12
Integer vitae:	*(Latin)* wholeness of life (from Horace's *Odes*, Book I, Ode 22)
a certain place . . . intentions:	proverb 'the road to hell is paved with good intentions'
Last day luridness:	at the end of the world it will be consumed by fire

---

Phase the Fifth · The Woman Pays · Chapter 35

Angel turns away from Tess; he feels that she is no longer the woman he loved. Despite her pleading he does not relent. He goes out for a walk and Tess follows; they hardly speak to one another. She puts herself entirely at his command. As night falls they go to separate beds.

COMMENTARY: An uneven chapter. Some of the dialogue between Tess and Angel does not convince us; it is artificially heightened with exclamations of 'O' and 'Ah', but often the structure of the sentences is more complex than people under great strain can use. It is the language of melodrama, not real life. At the same time, however, the observed details, such as Angel's tear, or the description of the forlorn walk, are powerful, and the indifference of nature and natural objects is well conveyed.

NOTES AND GLOSSARY:

exculpatory:	attempting to free from blame
chromatic:	to do with colour
auricular:	to do with the hearing
purblind:	dull, stupid
treadled:	moved his feet as if operating a machine
prestidigitation:	conjuring trick
good-hussif:	*(dialect)* bag for needlework things
***Agape*:**	*(Greek)* love-feast

'Behold when thy face . . . pain': Swinburne, *Atalanta in Calydon*
more sinned against than sinning: Shakespeare, *King Lear*, III.2
tester of white dimity: canopy of cotton cloth
misletoe: supposed to bring good luck and fertility
passion's slave: Shakespeare, *Hamlet*, III.2
The little less . . . away: Browning, 'By the Fireside'

Chapter 36

For the next three days Angel goes off each day to the mill. He is absolutely fixed in his purpose; he cannot acknowledge Tess as his wife while Alec lives, but will not divorce her. Tess hopes at times that continued life together will break down his resistance, but finally she suggests that she should return home for a while.

COMMENTARY: In this chapter Hardy preserves a distance from his characters, indicating faults on both sides, but refusing to judge. People are what they are, he seems to be saying.

NOTES AND GLOSSARY:

she sought not . . . provoked: from the Bible, I Corinthians 12:5
endure the ills . . . others: echo of Shakespeare, *Hamlet*, III.1
M. Sully-Prudhomme: (1839–97) French poet

vitalizations:	givings of life (implying children)
covenant:	formal agreement
boreal:	Northern

Chapter 37

In his sleep Angel carries Tess out of the house and lays her in an open coffin in the abbey grounds. The following morning, remembering nothing, he confirms his decision to part from her. They revisit Talbothays before they separate. Angel tells Tess not to attempt to see him. She returns home.

COMMENTARY: This chapter has been criticised for its improbability, but it tells us a great deal poetically about the way Angel imprisons his true feelings under the control of his reason, and about Tess's complete submissiveness.

NOTES AND GLOSSARY:
Samson shaking himself: from the Bible, Judges 16:20
fiasco: *(Italian)* disaster
'God's not ... world': a reversal of Browning's *Pippa Passes*: 'God's in his heaven,/All's right with the world'

Chapter 38

Tess returns home, but finds her parents unsympathetic; her mother calls her a fool, and her father only feels his ancestry has been insulted. Humiliated, and afraid of what others will say, Tess uses a letter from Angel as a pretext for leaving, pretending she is going to join him. She gives her mother half the money which Angel had left her.

COMMENTARY: The basic selfishness of Tess's parents is brought out here. When Tess talks at home she uses more dialect.

NOTES AND GLOSSARY:
'Nation: damnation
unceiled: without a ceiling
glane: *(dialect)* sneer

Chapter 39

Three weeks later Angel returns to his parents. He has decided to emigrate to Brazil, and uses this as an excuse for not having brought Tess with him, saying that he will do so when he goes to Brazil the second time. He lies to defend Tess, saying that she is pure and chaste. The conventional nature of Angel's prejudices is pointed out, and Hardy insists on Tess's essential purity.

COMMENTARY: This chapter shows the limited outlook of Angel's family. Angel's mother has the same idealisation of country girls as her son once had.

Hardy takes sides much more in this chapter, showing his own attitude to Angel and Tess more directly. (Angel's sensuousness, for example, emerges when he is alone in his room thinking of Tess.)

NOTES AND GLOSSARY:
Wiertz: (1806–65) painter specialising in morbid subjects. The museum is in Brussels
Van Beers: (1852–1927) Belgian painter
Pagan moralist: the Roman emperor Marcus Aurelius (AD 121–80)

the Nazarene: Jesus Christ (see John 14:27)
apostasy: abandonment of principles
a good thing ... Nazareth: from the Bible, John 1:46 (used of Christ)

Chapter 40

Angel prepares to leave, banking thirty pounds for Tess's future use. Returning to the house where they had stayed he meets Izz Huett, who tells him that all the girls who loved him have left the diary. Under the pressure of memories of Tess, and feeling the injustice of things, he asks Izz to go with him to Brazil. She agrees, but when she confesses that Tess loved him more than anyone, Angel changes his mind. He almost turns back to Tess, but continues on his course.

COMMENTARY: This chapter demonstrates the psychological tension in Angel. He is inconsistent in his moral attitudes under the pressure of emotion. This phase of the novel is called 'The Woman Pays' – and it is not only Tess, but the other dairymaids also who suffer.

NOTES AND GLOSSARY:
a parlous state: wretched condition (see Shakespeare, *As You Like It*, III.3)
the prophet: Balaam, who prophesied the future of the Israelites (see the Bible, Numbers 22–4)

Chapter 41

Eight months later Tess, after spending the summer in casual employment, is without a job. Her supply of money is gone – she sent part of the thirty pounds to her parents to repair their roof – and she is totally isolated. She sets out for a job with Marian, and she meets on the way the man who had insulted her in Chapter 33. Fleeing from him, she makes her bed in a wood where she is disturbed by strange noises which are explained the next morning when she finds birds left half-dead by a shooting party. She puts them out of their misery, and compares their plight to her own.

We hear briefly that all is not well with Angel in Brazil.

COMMENTARY: The comparison of Tess to a wild animal is fully developed in the comparison of her plight to that of the birds. But whereas they had no choice in their suffering, we see in this chapter how much Tess's fear of what others will think, and her pride, stop her from seeking help.

NOTES AND GLOSSARY:
relics: objects connected with a saint, held in veneration
éclat: *(French)* brilliant success

Chapter 42

Tess goes on her way, wearing her ugliest clothes to avoid the attentions of men. She fails to find employment until finally she reaches Flintcomb-Ash, where Marian now works. Here she is taken on for hard work on the land, concealing her married status.

COMMENTARY: Marian's comment 'it must be something outside of you both' is very like the attitude taken by Tess's father in Chapter 38.

Notice that Tess is now described as a fieldwoman – she has achieved a premature maturity.

NOTES AND GLOSSARY:

mommet: *(dialect)* scarecrow
'the maiden's mouth . . . head': from Swinburne's 'Fragoletta'
Cybele: classical goddess of nature, depicted as 'many-breasted' in sculpture
plashed down with the quickset: bent down and interwoven to form a thicker hedge
starve-acre: unfertile
Old Lady Day: Feast of the Annunciation; in the pre-1752 calendar on 6 April (still the beginning of the British financial year), now 25 March

Chapter 43

In harsh winter weather Tess and Marian work first outside, and then, when snow comes, inside at the hard task of reed-drawing. Izz Huett joins them. She tells Marian of Angel's offer to take her away, and Marian then relates it to Tess. Tess is upset, and begins to write a letter which she does not finish.

COMMENTARY: Much of the description is built up of very precisely observed details, and written in a style which involves much formality. This gives both life and gravity to the scene.

The technique of bringing back minor characters from earlier in the book (the girls who fought Tess just before the seduction, and the farmer who taunted her on her way) both reinforces the sense of things conspiring to bring about human misery and intensifies Tess's plight by reminding her both of Alec and Angel.

NOTES AND GLOSSARY:

lanchets or lynchets: *(dialect)* beds of flint
siliceous: quartz
cusped: pointed
hessian: a coarse cloth

the two Marys:	Mary, mother of Christ, and Mary Magdalene
integument:	skin, rind
salient:	jutting out
Aurora:	the *Aurora borealis* is a brilliant light effect in the region of the Poles
terraqueous:	of both water and earth
reed-drawing:	preparing straw for use in thatching roofs
achromatic:	without colour
Amazonian:	the Amazons were a legendary race of warrior women

thirtover, lackaday: *(dialect)* perverse, careless

Chapter 44

As the anniversary of her wedding approaches, Tess finally decides to go to Angel's parents to ask them for information. But at the end of the long walk she first finds the vicarage empty, and then, while waiting, overhears Angel's brothers and Mercy Chant discussing Angel's 'unfortunate marriage'. They also discover and take away the walking boots she had hidden when she put on her best shoes to approach the vicarage. In despair she turns away. On the way home she hears a preacher, who turns out to be Alec d'Urberville, converted to Christianity by Angel's father.

COMMENTARY: The way Izz and Marian dress Tess smartly for her journey recalls the efforts of her mother before she set out for Trantridge.

This is a chapter which aims at pathos, and perhaps succeeds almost too well. Hardy is in danger of over-doing things.

NOTES AND GLOSSARY:

cretaceous:	chalky
crape quilling:	crape (a kind of material) closely pleated
hogs'-backs:	hills shaped like pigs' backs
guindée:	*(French)* stiff, prim
Publicans and Sinners:	in the Bible, despised groups of people
Scribes and Pharisees:	religious leaders, often presented in the New Testament as self-righteous
ranter:	vehement preacher (often of an extreme sect)
dialectician:	logical arguer
'O foolish Galatians ... ':	from the Bible, Galatians 3:1

Phase the Sixth · The Convert · Chapter 45

Alec sees Tess as she leaves, and falters in his preaching. He catches her up on the road, and explains his conversion. She, taught by Angel, cannot accept his beliefs. Before he leaves he makes her swear on the strange stone, the 'Cross in Hand', that she will not tempt him. A passer-by reveals to her that this is not a holy stone, but hides the bones of a wicked man.

COMMENTARY: Hardy tries very hard to make Alec's conversion convincing, both by showing his old character underneath the new, and by the way he makes Alec use inappropriate language – 'a jolly new idea'. Notice Alec's continued selfishness – he blames Tess for tempting him.

NOTES AND GLOSSARY:

bizarrerie: *(French)* strangeness
Paulinism: following the teaching of St Paul
Cyprian image: image of Venus, goddess of love
Methodist: followers of John Wesley (1703–91), who broke away from the Anglican Church (which is linked to the State), are called by this name
'Come out ... Lord': from the Bible, 2 Corinthians 6:17
wuld: *(dialect)* old
petite mort: *(French)* faintness

Chapter 46

Alec interrupts Tess's work and asks her to marry him. She refuses, telling him finally that she is already married. Disturbed by this encounter she writes to Angel, though again she does not finish the letter. Alec returns to her at her lodging, having broken a preaching engagement. She presents to him some of the arguments against his beliefs which she had learnt from Angel.

COMMENTARY: There are parallels between Alec and Angel – Alec is thinking of emigrating – a thing Angel had done earlier; he threatens the farmer, a thing Angel had also done earlier. This helps to keep both characters in the reader's mind.

NOTES AND GLOSSARY:

'The unbelieving ... husband': from the Bible, 1 Corinthians 7:14
Candlemas Fair: 2 February
Sermon on the Mount: Christ's teaching of love (Matthew 5–7)
syllogism: form of reasoning by strict deduction
Dictionnaire Philosophique: (1764) by Voltaire (1694–1778)
Huxley's *Essays*: leading defence of Darwin's (1809–82) theories
like the devils ... tremble: from the Bible, James 2:19
servants of corruption: from the Bible, 2 Peter 2:19–20
witch of Babylon: the horrendous figure in the Bible, Revelation 17

Chapter 47

While Tess is working on the steam threshing-machine Alec, dressed in ordinary clothes, approaches. During the dinner-break he tells Tess that as a result of their previous conversation he has lost his religious enthusiasm. He tries to persuade Tess to come with him, but when she strikes him viciously he leaves, saying he will return later in the day.

COMMENTARY: The steam-threshing machine epitomises the agricultural revolution, men replaced by machines under the control of people who have no feeling for the land. Hardy makes this machine seem more unpleasant by giving it active, human qualities, and, by using long and unfamiliar words in his description of it, emphasises its significance.

NOTES AND GLOSSARY:

primum mobile: *(Latin)* 'first mover'; that which sets the world in motion
aborigines: used in the strict Latinate sense 'those there from the beginning'
Tophet: a place where fire was kept burning (see the Bible, Isaiah 30:33)
steam threshing-machine: they were introduced in England in the 1840s
Plutonic: Pluto was Roman god of hell
autochthonous: native
stooded: stuck
hagrode: *(dialect)* bewitched
Weltlust: *(German)* delight in the world
Hymenaeus and Alexander: see the Bible, 1 Timothy 1:19–20
bachelor-apostle: St Paul
words of . . . Hosea: Hosea 2:7
skimmer-cake: *(dialect)* kind of pancake

Chapter 48

As work continues Alec returns, and speaks to Tess again at the end of the day, offering to look after her family. She again refuses him, but is worried at what she is pressed to do, and writes a long and impassioned letter to Angel, asking him to come to her.

COMMENTARY: As the work is finishing rats are driven from the straw and killed – an image which has something in common with Alec's persecution of Tess.

Tess's letter is perhaps rather well-written (though Hardy is careful to include some non-standard expressions like 'how it do hurt') but the turmoil of her feelings is well caught.

NOTES AND GLOSSARY:

mammet-time:	*(dialect)* a break for refreshment mid-morning or afternoon
faeces:	*(Latin)* animal excrement
Jacob's ladder:	seen in a dream leading from earth to heaven (see the Bible, Genesis 28:10–13)
Pandemonium:	the city of the devils in Hell in Milton's *Paradise Lost*

Chapter 49

Tess's letter is forwarded by Angel's parents, though it does not reach him for a long time, for he is having a hard time in Brazil. There, partly as a result of his meditations on his own situation, partly through the arguments of a briefly-met friend, he questions his former actions, and feels afresh his love for Tess. She meanwhile thinks rather hopelessly of what she will do if he does return. Suddenly her sister, Liza-Lu, arrives with the news that her mother is seriously ill, and she sets off home.

COMMENTARY: Angel's experiences have matured him. Hardy hammers home his view of 'the universal harshness'.

The sense of things conspiring against Tess is strengthened by the way we hear in the chapter of her family's difficulties immediately after Alec has put pressure on Tess by offering to help them.

NOTES AND GLOSSARY:

as Abraham . . . together:	Abraham was ordered by God to sacrifice his son, Isaac (Genesis 22:1–14)
Hellenic Paganism:	the philosophy of Greece
the gleaning of grapes . . . Abi-ezer:	see the Bible, Judges 8:1–3
traipsing:	tramping
drave:	toil
withy-basket:	basket made of plaited strips of willow

Chapter 50

Tess nurses her mother and tends the neglected garden, where one day Alec appears dressed as agricultural labourer. He again offers to help, and though Tess rejects him she blurts out 'I have no husband', believing now that she will not see Angel again. When she returns home she finds that her father has suddenly died, and consequently the family will have to leave the house.

COMMENTARY: In the opening paragraphs, we see things through Tess's eyes (in contrast to the detached descriptions elsewhere).

Two strains of imagery come together in this chapter; the fire which

LEEDS METROPOLITAN UNIVERSITY LIBRARY

has often accompanied Tess's darker moments, and the recollections of the Genesis story.

NOTES AND GLOSSARY:

turnpike-roads:	main roads (upon which a toll was paid)
pricking and ducking:	in earlier times suspected witches were tested by people sticking needles into them and by ducking them in water
whickered:	*(dialect)* sniggered, tittered
hired labour:	paid work for the farmer
couch-grass:	a persistent weedy grass
pillar of a cloud:	which went in front of the Israelites (see the Bible, Exodus 13:21)
Other One:	the Devil
scene of Milton's:	*Paradise Lost* IX.626–31, where Satan tempts Eve
'liviers':	people whose tenure of property depended upon the life of the tenant
determined:	reached its end
Olympians:	very important people (Olympus was the home of the classical gods)

Chapter 51

The Durbeyfield family have to leave; Tess blames herself, because her reputation in the village prevented her mother being allowed to stay. While she is on her own in the house Alec appears and offers to take the family in at Trantridge. Tess refuses, but in despair writes a note to Angel blaming him for his cruelty. She feels that physically Alec *is* her husband. She promises to tell her mother of Alec's offer when they arrive at Kingsbere.

COMMENTARY: Even in village society there are those who insist upon conventional moral standards. Notice how Tess blames herself here, as she had at the time of the horse's death, for the sufferings of her family.

NOTES AND GLOSSARY:

Egypt. . . Land of Promise: the Israelites were led from captivity in Egypt to the 'Promised Land' (see Exodus)

'Not in utter nakedness . . . come': from Wordsworth's 'Ode on Intimations of Immortality'

Chapter 52

The family set out (meeting Marian and Izz, also journeying to new jobs), but when they arrive at Kingsbere they find their lodgings have been let. They leave their belongings in the churchyard, near the tombs of their ancestors. Tess suddenly meets Alec, lying in the church on one of the tombs. Again she sends him away, but wishes she were dead. Meanwhile Marian and Izz think of Tess, and a month later write anonymously to Angel, warning him that Tess is in danger.

COMMENTARY: The motif of the decayed family reaches its peak here, especially in the symbolic (and frightening) presence of the false d'Urberville on the tombs of the true family.

NOTES AND GLOSSARY:
the hexagon to the bee: bees build six-sided cells for their honey
dresser: kitchen sideboard for crockery etc.
Ark of the Covenant: religious symbol of the Israelites
superincumbent: lying on top
deparked: converted from being the grounds of a great house
stale: urinate
brasses: memorial tablets, mounted in stone on tombs or walls
Ostium sepulchri ... *d'Urberville*: doorway to the tomb of the ancient d'Urberville family
the old order changeth: from Tennyson's *Morte d'Arthur*
tole: *(dialect)* entice

Phase the Seventh · Fulfilment · Chapter 53

Angel returns, much altered by his ordeals. He receives Tess's second note, and determines to seek her out. He receives a brief note in reply to a letter to Joan, telling him that Tess is away. Just before he sets out he receives the letter from Marian and Izz.

COMMENTARY: The detail in the first meeting of Angel and his parents gives solidity and liveliness to the scene.

In this chapter neither the reader nor Angel knows exactly what has happened to Tess, thus increasing the suspense.

NOTES AND GLOSSARY:
the Word: used in the Bible for God
Crivell's dead *Christus*: fifteenth-century painting of the crucified Christ
'which alters ... finds': Shakespeare, *Sonnets* No.116
Faustina: debauched wife of Marcus Aurelius (AD121–80).
Cornelia: virtuous wife of Pompey (106–48BC)
Lucretia: virtuous woman raped by Tarquin (534–510BC)
Phryne: notorious Greek prostitute (fourth century BC)
the woman taken ... stoned: a sinner pardoned by Christ (John 8)
wife of Uriah: Bathsheba, seduced by King David, who later married her

Chapter 54

Angel traces Tess, from Flintcomb-Ash to Marlott, where nothing remains but the grave of John Durbeyfield – for which Angel pays the bill – and then to Kingsbere where Joan tells him reluctantly that Tess is at Sandbourne.

COMMENTARY: There are links with the past, as Angel retraces Tess's paths. His feelings about the house, now not lived in by Tess, contrast with his view of the farmhouse at Talbothays in the days of their happiness (Chapter 25). Angel's search parallels the earlier quest of Alec, who had traced her from Flintcomb-Ash.

NOTES AND GLOSSARY:
a tale told by an idiot: Shakespeare, *Macbeth* V.5

Chapter 55

Angel finds Tess, living as Alec's wife at a lodging-house in fashionable Sandbourne. She tells him he has come too late, for Alec's kindness to her family won her back, although she now hates him because he had asserted that Angel would never return.

COMMENTARY: The novelty of urban Sandbourne is stressed; it is an unnatural environment for the country girl.

Tess being dressed in fine clothes fulfils the offer Alec had made when she first left him to clothe her 'in the best' (Chapter 12).

The poignancy of this meeting is increased by the mention of the 'fluty voice' which had first attracted Angel, and by the ironic fact that her spirit and body are indeed now separated, as she had said they could be in the first conversation he overheard (Chapter 18).

NOTES AND GLOSSARY:
the prophet's gourd: see the Bible, Jonah 4:5–10

Chapter 56

Mrs Brooks, the landlady, having overheard Tess and Angel, goes upstairs and sees through the keyhole an argument between Tess and Alec. Tess goes out and suddenly Mrs Brooks sees a bloodstain spreading on the ceiling. She calls in a workman, and they discover Alec's dead body.

COMMENTARY: Hardy gains a narrative detachment in this scene by presenting it through the eyes of an outsider.

NOTES AND GLOSSARY:

some Ixionian wheel: in classical mythology Ixion was condemned in Hell to be bound to an ever-turning fiery wheel

wafer: small disc of sealing-wax

Chapter 57

Waiting for a train from Sandbourne, Angel takes a walk, and is overtaken by Tess, who tells him that she has murdered Alec. Angel is amazed, but determined to protect her. They wander together 'like two small children', forgetting the crime, until finally they find an empty house into which they creep.

COMMENTARY: Though Angel and Tess are reunited, and find 'rest at last', Hardy never lets us forget that a crime has been committed. Notice that Tess is spurred to murder by Alec's calling Angel 'a foul name', just as Angel had struck Farmer Groby for the same offence to Tess.

The darkness without a candle in which they spend their first happy night is ominous, and gains its power because of the understatement Hardy employs.

NOTES AND GLOSSARY:

Antinous: beautiful youth, beloved of the Emperor Hadrian

Apollo: classical god of music and the sun; a type of beauty

Atalanta's race: legendary woman, who would only marry a man who could defeat her in a race

Chapter 58

After a week in the house, where Tess wishes to stay despite Angel's anxiety to escape, the caretaker discovers them sleeping. Though she does not disturb them they feel they have been noticed, and so set out. At night they reach Stonehenge, where they sleep after Tess has asked Angel to look after, even to marry, her sister 'Liza-Lu if anything should happen to her. At dawn they are surrounded by the police, who wait till Tess awakes before taking her away.

COMMENTARY: This chapter is packed with symbolic detail – especially Tess being found in the place of a religion older than almost any other.

Notice how Tess's breathing is like an animal's – the last of many such comparisons.

Hardy's mastery of narrative technique shows in this chapter in his management of alternating movement, dialogue and stillness. The poignancy is increased by the repeated motif of the peacefully sleeping being overlooked first by the caretaker, then the police.

NOTES AND GLOSSARY:

contiguous;	neighbouring
architrave:	overhead beam
trilithon:	two vertical stones supporting a third laid across them
greater than himself:	Christ, who gave no answer to Pilate's question 'what is truth' (John 19:9)
reared:	roused

Chapter 59

At eight a.m. Angel and 'Liza-Lu ascend a hill from which they overlook the prison. A black flag signifies that Tess has been executed. They go on hand in hand.

COMMENTARY: The presence of 'Liza-Lu in this final episode is often criticised as sentimental, but Hardy was always fascinated by the idea of a man falling in love with more than one member of a family. It forms the basis of his novel *The Wellbeloved*, and perhaps derives from his own feelings towards his three cousins.

The austerity of this final scene is largely created by the complete detachment with which Hardy writes, and the masterly control of the rhythm of the sentences.

NOTES AND GLOSSARY:

Giotto:	(1267–1337) Italian painter
isometric:	of equal measurement
hospice:	Hospital of St Cross in Winchester, which supplied bread and ale to all applicants
Gothic:	of the later middle ages – about 1250–1550
in Aeschylean phrase:	a translation of a line from the Greek tragedian's *Prometheus*. Hardy maintained that it did not imply he believed in an actively malicious god, but was a metaphorical phrase
joined hands again:	perhaps a recollection of the closing lines of Milton's *Paradise Lost* where Adam and Eve: '. . . hand in hand with wandering steps and slow,/Through Eden took their solitary way'

Part 3

Commentary

Characters

Several different sorts of things have to be taken into account when building up a picture of a character.

(a) What the character does and says.
(b) What other characters say about him or her.
(c) The things the novelist himself says.
(d) Other information about the character's circumstances.

But what a character is 'like' as an individual is only part of the picture. It is also necessary to consider how the character is used by the novelist in the various patterns of the book as a whole. So the critic must also take into account:

(a) Whether we are meant to sea a character as embodying characteristics that make him stand for a whole type of class of people.
(b) What the relationship is between one character and another; if for example, two characters are deliberately contrasted.
(c) What kinds of influence one character has over another.
(d) How any one character fits into the pattern of themes in the novel.

This is by no means a complete list, but it is necessary that a student should not be content merely to consider the characters in a novel as if they were real people. Obviously some characters exist mainly to serve a functional role; they have only a limited life, though in the best writing the novelist is careful to give them enough character to make them believable. These minor characters form a kind of background against which the major characters enact their drama, and help to convey to the reader a sense of a whole world. It is therefore sensible to begin the consideration of the characters in *Tess* with some of these simpler figures.

Tess's family

Tess's father and mother are of a social class 'ranking distinctly above' the agricultural labourer (Chapter 51). But it is clear that Jack Durbeyfield makes little effort to maintain his family in comfort.

Though 'he had good strength to work at times', 'the times could not be relied on to coincide with the hours of requirement' (Chapter 5). His wife, Joan, is little better, letting domestic chores 'linger on to the end of the week'. With the pressures of bringing up a large family in difficult circumstances, it is no wonder that both of them prefer slipping out for a drink, when they can forget their cares, to doing anything very positive.

Their characters are most fully developed in their attitudes to two things: their ancestry and their children, especially Tess. Jack shows a childish pride in the discovery of his descent, and initially there is some good-humoured fun at his expense. But as the story develops the consequences have to be taken more seriously. His sense of his own dignity prevents him from getting a job (Chapter 49), and he comes to see everything that happens in terms of his 'high family': Tess's illegitimate child is a 'smudge . . . upon that nobility', and so he locks the door to prevent her fetching a parson (Chapter 14); the failure of her marriage only worries him because of what others will think of this collapse of his family pride. The futility of the obsession is clearly shown in his absurd idea of getting antiquarians to keep him when his wife is ill (Chapter 50), but Hardy shows its pathos in the inscription on the tomb (Chapter 54).

The d'Urberville ancestry does affect Joan, but her ambitions are much simpler – she wants her daughter to rise in the world by making a successful marriage. She is, therefore, very concerned at the impression Tess is going to make on her Trantridge 'kinsfolk', and insists on dressing her up. But the superficiality of her attitude is shown very clearly in her lack of moral concern for Tess's welfare. We sympathise with Tess's accusing questions after her return: 'Why didn't you tell me there was danger in men-folk?' (Chapter 13), and recognise in her answer both her calculating, shrewd simple-mindedness and also her readiness to put up with whatever happens: 'Well, we must make the best of it, I suppose'. Tess herself later recognises 'how light was the touch of events the most oppressive upon Mrs Durbeyfield's elastic spirit' (Chapter 31).

Hardy uses the dialect speech of the Durbeyfield family to fix them very firmly in a specific social class and region. Their function in the book is to serve three main ends:

(1) Through them the theme of the decline of a family is given immediate dramatic life, for not only has the d'Urberville family declined in the centuries before the book begins, but we witness the final stage of their collapse during the course of the novel.

(2) Hardy helps us to understand the character of Tess more fully by presenting the context in which she was brought up, showing us various aspects of her character which she inherited from her parents.

(3) Tess's sense of responsibility for her family is one of the book's most important structural elements. At almost every stage of her life it is her concern for her family which influences her actions, right up to her final decision to return to Alec.

Angel's family

This family is much less richly drawn than Tess's, but still Hardy distinguishes between the parents, with their rigid Evangelical faith, but fundamental charity to their fellow human beings, and the liberalism of thought, but restricted feeling, of Angel's brothers.

The family is middle-class, and the parents show concern at Angel's choosing to marry a country girl. But at the same time they, like their son, are capable of holding an idealised picture of country innocence, and we are told that Tess was wrong to estimate her father-in-law by his sons (Chapter 44). They, from their first remarks to their last, show a far greater intolerance of people of a lower class than themselves.

The function of the Clare family in the novel has two main strands:

(1) They stand for the limited moral values of the Christian middle-class, by which Tess feels herself condemned.
(2) Their presentation helps us to understand, and to believe, Angel's relapse into conventional values when faced by Tess's confession.

The rural characters

Compared with many of Hardy's other novels, *Tess* has few minor characters of this sort. They can be divided roughly into three groups:

(1) The least obvious, the narrow-minded moralists. Represented perhaps by the man with the pot of red paint, it is they who force Tess's family to leave Marlott after the death of Jack, because they are offended by Tess's past.
(2) The drunken, rough characters who frequent Rolliver's, and have their counterparts in the villagers of Trantridge. Two of that group, the Queens of Diamonds and Spades, recur at Flintcomb-Ash, where they are unnaturally strong and mannish. There is a moral coarseness about this group, shown by the laughter as Alec carries Tess away (Chapter 10). Oddly, though, Hardy consistently uses striking mythological and spiritual imagery to describe this group, both during the Chaseborough dance (Chapter 10), and as they make their drunken way home. Hardy here seems to be suggesting both the power of drunken illusion, and yet at the same time to be insisting on their kinship with something essential and pagan in human character.

(3) The other characters are the inhabitants of Talbothays, described as living in almost the ideal way (Chapter 20). The dairymaids are generous and fatalistic in accepting that Tess is favoured by Angel, but at the same time they suffer under the 'emotion thrust on them by cruel Nature's law' (Chapter 23). There are two main functions to this group: (*a*) In the early days at Talbothays they are used to build up an idyllic rural picture. (*b*) Their experiences show that Tess endures only the most extreme consequences of feelings which affect everyone. Their lives are less complicated than hers, but not a lot less painful. This helps us to accept that what Tess goes through is not just a special, individual case.

If we take them all together, then Hardy seems to be showing that the country folk are indeed not to be classed together as 'the pitiable dummy known as Hodge' (Chapter 18), but have their own variety of feelings and attitudes. Through these characters Hardy is able to introduce naturally the country stories and superstitions which contribute so much to the novel's individual character.

Alec d'Urberville

Alec comes from a newly-rich family, which has tried to gain social status by adopting an old name (Chapter 5). His easy access to money colours the way he reacts to things – his only reaction to his sense of the wrong he has done to Tess is to say 'I will pay to the uttermost farthing' (Chapter 12).

His main characteristics may be summed up as: (*i*) selfishness, (*ii*) arrogance, and bad temper, and (*iii*) capriciousness and superficiality of feeling.

(1) His selfishness is shown clearly by the way he always blames Tess for his own failings. Just before he rapes her he says 'For near three mortal months have *you* trifled with *my* feelings' (Chapter 11); he later blames her parents (Chapter 46), and asks Tess to swear on the Cross in Hand never to tempt *him* (Chapter 45).
(2) His arrogance and bad temper frequently rise to the surface, from his early desire for a kiss of *mastery*, to the anger that surfaces when he learns that Tess is married.
(3) His capriciousness has to be convincing if we are to believe in his conversion. Hardy prepares the reader early, by calling him 'capriciously passionate' (Chapter 8), and reminds us of the quality in a later scene, where his concern for Tess is described as 'capricious compunction' (Chapter 46).

But obviously, if we are to believe that Tess would live with him for a time after her seduction, then Hardy has to give Alec some good qualities. He has a dashing appearance (see Chapter 7), and we find that Tess hesitates to say absolutely that she always finds his love-making offensive (Chapter 11). She later says that her 'eyes were dazed' by him for a little while (Chapter 12). Perhaps it is the reticence about sexuality at Hardy's time which makes this side of Alec's character less than completely convincing, perhaps it is simply the rather melodramatic way he writes, but many readers find it difficult to see a better side to Alec, even though his interest in Tess is longer-lasting than his previous affairs, and he does offer to marry her.

The great problem, however, is his brief conversion to evangelical Christianity. Hardy could, after all, have arranged for Tess to meet Alec again in any number of natural ways. In order to understand why Hardy chose this dramatic device, Alec's place in the pattern of the book has to be considered:

(1) The ease with which Alec is converted and then retracts are symptomatic of the failure of Christianity to make any real impact on the modern, mercantile world.

(2) Throughout the work Alec is contrasted specifically with Angel – they are the two men who expose Tess to the opposing experiences of lust and love. They are both men of the new world, but their essential difference is exposed by Angel's rigidly intellectual rejection of the old faith compared with Alec's facile acceptance. One is a man of reason, the other of emotion.

(3) The conversion, in which Alec adopts the dress of the Methodist, is but one of a series of disguises he takes on, culminating in his appearance to Tess 'in a gathered smockfrock, such as was now only worn by the most old-fashioned of the labourers' (Chapter 50). This disguising links him, as he himself suggests, to Satan, the tempter of Eve and mankind, who, in the Bible, continually assumes different shapes. It also emphasises the fact that Alec belongs nowhere. His house is new, set in the age-old forest, and he meets his death in the newly-sprouted town of Sandbourne. (It is also appropriate, therefore, that he shows his final mastery of Tess by dressing *her* up in clothes which are unnatural to her.)

All this may explain *why* Hardy chose this device, but it does not necessarily prove that it is convincing; on that question each reader must make up his own mind.

Angel Clare

Angel is the first character to be considered who has any real complexity about him. The reader's sense of the richness of the character results from two rather different things, which need to be treated separately.

(1) He is a man whose personality is torn by conflicts. He is capable of thinking and feeling differently at different times, for though he places all his faith in his intellect and reason, he falls prey both to his passions and to his irrational, inherited prejudices. The moment which focuses these conflicts for the reader is his rejection of Tess on their wedding night.

(2) At the same time Angel is a person who develops towards maturity throughout the novel. He changes fundamentally (as Alec does not), and in this experience his rejection of Tess is only a stepping-stone to his fuller understanding of himself and the world.

(1) The first time Angel is heard speaking at Talbothays he sounds very much like a self-conscious intellectual. He says 'It's a curious story; it carries us back to medieval times, when faith was a living thing' (Chapter 17). This is indeed a 'singular remark for a dairy-yard', but fairly representative of a tone of voice we hear from him throughout the book. Angel is a man who believes in the importance of the intellect, and only trusts what his reason approves. It is this quality which has led him to reject Christianity, and which prevents his turning back to Tess.

But for all his belief in principles, his conduct towards Tess is shown to be inconsistent. He expects her to forgive him, but is not prepared to show the same charity towards her. Hardy gives three main reasons for his conduct. The first is that he was 'the slave to custom and conventionality when surprised back into his early teachings' (Chapter 39). Hardy convinces us of the truth of this statement by giving a lot of other evidence of Angel's conventional middle-class values. He wishes to 'improve' Tess before taking her to visit his family; he is attracted by Tess's ancestry although intellectually he despises it; in his extreme anger with Tess he says 'You almost make me say you are an unapprehending peasant woman' (Chapter 35).

The second reason is that though he rejects the 'lady' his parents want him to marry, and wishes to choose a girl who can help in his farming career, yet he unconsciously idealises the life and the class of people with whom he allies himself. Though he quickly learns that country people are not the dumb, stupid Hodge of one kind of literary caricature, yet he talks of Tess to his mother as being 'brimful of poetry – actualised poetry' (Chapter 26). He has substituted a literary, unreal picture of rural innocence for the picture he had earlier discarded.

Angel, Hardy tells us, loved with feelings 'more spiritual than animal'; he 'could love desperately, but with a love more especially inclined to the imaginative and ethereal' (Chapter 31). This is the third reason for his actions. It is here, of course, that he contrasts most specifically with Alec, whose love is animal, not spiritual. For such a lover 'corporeal presence is sometimes less appealing than corporeal absence' (Chapter 36). It is understandable, then, that a man feeling in this kind of way should experience a profound shock when confronted with the fact that his wife has already known the physical side of love. It is almost an offence to his own lack of physical desire.

These are the reasons for his rejection, but Hardy makes clear, mainly through the sleepwalking scene (Chapter 37), that underneath these various different layers of inhibition there is genuine feeling and passion which Angel cannot bring himself to own when waking. Indeed, it is suggested, when he sees Tess finally disappearing to her parents, that 'he hardly knew that he loved her still' (Chapter 37). It takes the experiences of Brazil for him to learn to understand and be truthful to himself.

(2) This brings us to the other aspect of Angel's character. When he is first introduced he is described as a student 'of something and everything' (Chapter 2). He is a man trying to learn, and this process is not completed until the very end of the book. He went to the dairy not only to learn about farming, but also 'as to a place from which as from a screened alcove he could calmly view the absorbing world without' (Chapter 25). This detachment does not last as he notices and gradually falls in love with Tess. The story of his life thereafter is of the slow and painful process of reconciling the safety of uninvolved detachment with the demands of his own feelings which drive him into contact with other people. When he leaves Tess 'The picture of life had changed for him. Before this time he had known it but speculatively; now he thought he knew it as a practical man; though perhaps he did not, even yet.' (Chapter 39). Hardy unambiguously makes the reader aware that Angel still has much to learn. It is when real suffering hits Angel in Brazil that he becomes aware for the first time of the limitations both of his intellectual ideas and of the emotional prejudices he had never recognised before. When he returns, therefore, though he is shocked at the murder of Alec, he can offer Tess his love without reservation.

The way in which Hardy introduces this story of Angel's maturation alongside the main story of Tess gives the novel variety. At the same time the fact that Angel is a subsidiary character, absent for a large part of the story, means that the narrative of his development is rather cramped. Though we can see what Hardy was aiming at, it may well be that he was not completely successful. Certainly many critics dismiss Angel as a 'prig'. Every reader must make up his or her own mind on this point.

Tess

As Tess is the book's central character there is a greater richness of information about her than any other. From her story are developed the novel's main themes; from the reader's identification with her suffering come the strongest emotions. It is therefore difficult to write about her character without recounting virtually everything about the book, though her character is basically a simple one. It consists of:

(1) Her physical attractiveness.
(2) The mixing in her personality of the apparently contradictory qualities of pride and independence of spirit with a passivity and submissiveness towards other people and her fate.
(3) Her instinctive identity with the natural world of feelings and emotions, which is overlaid by a conventional morality.

(1) Her beauty as she grows from a deceptively mature girl to a young woman of twenty or so is continually stressed. Hardy emphasises especially the attractiveness of her eyes (which so torment Alec), and her fluty voice (which first attracts Angel, and is poignantly recalled by him in Chapter 39). Her beauty becomes a burden to her, and the scene of her voluntary disfigurement is especially poignant (Chapter 42). Tess is brought physically to life for the reader to a much greater extent than any other character.

(2) That Tess is capable of pride and independence is shown repeatedly throughout the book; in her determination in leaving Alec, her unwillingness to tell her parents the truth about her marriage or to approach Angel's parents. It is this pride which prevents her from trying to win Angel back by staging an emotional scene. Hardy links this pride very specifically to the apparently opposite side of her character: 'Pride, too, entered into her submission – which perhaps was a symptom of that reckless acquiescence in chance, too apparent in the whole d'Urberville family' (Chapter 37). He is saying that what we take to be submissiveness is often a lack of forethought, a willingness to take whatever may come. She derives this characteristic from her parents, but shares it with other rural characters.

Tess is not only submissive before events, but also to people; to Alec, and to Angel – she says to him 'I will obey you like your wretched slave' (Chapter 35). But yet she can and does show anger – when she strikes Alec (Chapter 47), or when she finally writes her anguished second letter to Angel (Chapter 51). It is this blending of opposing characteristics which helps to make Tess a credible character, while at the same time making clear that she is partly responsible for what happens to her. She has a heroic quality of endurance, of 'patience, that blending of moral courage with physical timidity' (Chapter 43), which does not obscure her flaws.

(3) The qualities so far discussed are presented mainly through Tess's actions and speech or else by the author's comments, but Hardy creates

the reader's sense of her kinship with Nature principally by the more indirect means of imagery and suggestion.

Early on we are told that Tess was 'a mere vessel of emotion untinctured by experience' (Chapter 2); later, though she has endured much, she is still 'a vessel of emotions rather than reasons' (Chapter 47). It is this instinctive, emotional quality which Hardy creates, mainly by continually comparing her with animal life. In his description of her as she is seen by Angel, she 'was warm as a sunned cat' (Chapter 27), and many other examples could be given. She is at one, also, with inanimate nature, 'a figure which is part of the landscape' (Chapter 42).

These are not just ways of telling the reader what Tess looks like, for Tess's suffering is repeatedly associated with animal suffering, at harvest or after pheasant-shooting. Hardy's insistence on images drawn from nature builds up to the moment when Tess is arrested, and her breathing is 'like that of a lesser creature than a woman' (Chapter 58). Our pity for Tess is therefore increased, we are made aware of how she is a victim, as all animal creation is, of external and uncomprehended forces.

But Tess is also linked with nature in 'the appetite for joy which pervades all creation' (Chapter 30). Her moral values are those of the natural world; she believes in the ever-present possibility of regeneration. She has, however, received an education, and has absorbed the values of Christianity and convention. Hardy asserts that 'most of the misery had been caused by her conventional aspect' (Chapter 14). Certainly it is her upbringing which makes her feel guilt at the birth of her child, which allows her to accept so completely Angel's verdict on her, and which persuades her that there was a moral validity in her association with Alec.

Of course, Tess's tragedy results mainly because of the imposition of conventional values on her by other people, but her suffering would not have been so intense if she had not, with part of her, acknowledged those values.

Unlike Angel, Tess does not change fundamentally throughout the book; she endures rather than initiates action. But as the story progresses the reader is drawn to a very full understanding of her character, and recognises a credible personality because of the wealth of detail which Hardy gives for each aspect of his heroine.

Themes

It is possible, when studying a novel, to single out various things with which the writer is concerned and discuss each under a separate heading. In Part 4 the student will find questions which lead him in this direction. But the relationship between the various major concerns of the book should also be understood – after all, the novelist could simply have written a treatise if all he wanted was to put across his ideas about things – and that is the main aim of this section.

Tess of the d'Urbervilles ends with the death of the heroine. Earlier in her story she had 'put her hand to her brow, and felt its curve, and the edges of her eye-sockets perceptible under the soft skin, and thought as she did so that a time would come when that bone would be bare' (Chapter 41). Angel realises his responsibility in intruding upon 'the single opportunity of existence ever vouchsafed to Tess' (Chapter 25). Thus Hardy stresses the fact that every individual life is precious, and also emphasises the inevitability of death.

This individual life of growth and decay takes place amongst other, larger patterns of 'flux and reflux – the rhythm of change' which 'alternate and persist in everything under the sky' (Chapter 50). The decay of the d'Urberville family and the brief glory of the gnats who shimmer across the lovers' path (Chapter 32) are part of the same inevitable process.

Individual life and the world about it are linked in their brevity but they are also identical in the 'inherent will to enjoy' (Chapter 43). After the death of her child, Tess's 'spirit within her rose automatically as the sap in the twigs. It was . . . the invincible instinct towards self-delight.' (Chapter 15). It is the inevitable struggle between mortality and the will to live which is the fundamental theme of the novel; the way in which Hardy links and contrasts the life of the individual with larger patterns is the fundamental means of expressing that theme.

The theme is perhaps most powerfully expressed when, at the end of the novel, though Angel presses Tess to escape, she is content to rest at Stonehenge and greets those who come to arrest her with the words: 'It is as it should be . . . This happiness could not have lasted.' (Chapter 58). At the end of her life, she has apparently reconciled the conflict. But this resolution comes about after much suffering, and in expressing and accounting for Tess's pain Hardy shows in many different ways how the individual's life is determined only partly by his or her own efforts, and how much depends upon the pressure of things over which the individual has no control.

Tess does not want to learn about history, which she feels will only show her 'that your nature and your past doings have been just like thousands' and thousands', and that your coming life and doings 'll be like thousands' and thousands'.' (Chapter 19). She is actually recognising what we have called the novel's fundamental theme, but what she does not recognise is that though she may want to ignore history, her history will not ignore her. We have already seen how much of her character is determined by the fact that she comes from the decayed family of the d'Urbervilles, and Hardy insists throughout the novel in many ways on the way present life is conditioned by the past.

This is true of the lives of whole communities as well as individuals. The nature of the soil on which people work, the lay-out of villages, as well as customs like club-walking are all part of the inevitable pressure of the past on the present. Hardy often includes some details about history in his descriptions of places.

In the novel three distinct layers of the past are distinguished. The remote pagan time of the Druids; the age when Christianity served the world well, and the modern age. In different ways Tess is affected by all three. Her remote ancestor is, appropriately, called Sir *Pagan* d'Urberville, and her kinship is emphasised by her sense of peace at the pagan place of Stonehenge. She professes a sort of Christian faith, though, as we have seen, in many ways it is conventional Christian morality which accounts for much of her suffering. Finally, in different ways, the two men who affect her life are representative of the modern age. Alec is a new kind of d'Urberville, from an industrial, not an agricultural life, having his home in new and novel places; modern also in his lack of any sense of belonging, whereas Angel's modernity is intellectual; he no longer believes in a Benificent Power. Tess, says Hardy, in many ways shares Angel's feelings, although she cannot use any but his words; she expresses the 'ache of modernism' (Chapter 19) indirectly. Though Hardy himself agreed intellectually with Angel, yet he also realises what had been lost, as when he describes the way chronic melancholy disappears under the influence of rural life (Chapter 18). We see in Tess's story the way all these layers conflict one with the other – and over none of them does Tess herself have any kind of control.

Within the smaller scale of events which makes up Tess's story the same kind of pressure of past upon present is everywhere apparent. She hopes forlornly that she might be able to escape from anyone who knew about her past by going to Talbothays, but she realises when she sees Alec again that 'the break of continuity between her earlier and present existence, which she had hoped for had not, after all, taken place. Bygones would never be complete bygones till she was a bygone herself.' (Chapter 45). Indeed those past events have never left her own consciousness. Thus Hardy demonstrates the way in which past and present are interwoven both on the grand scale and within the life of the individual.

In a work of any complexity, different motifs are used in various ways. We have just seen how conventional values form part of the pressure of Tess's inheritance upon her life. At the same time society's morality is contrasted in the novel as a whole with the more instinctive values of nature. It might seem at first sight that Hardy is simply saying that 'it is better to be natural'. But natural processes involve suffering and death, so the matter is not really as simple as that.

There are many images of nature distorted by man, which do suggest the way in which Hardy considered social convention perverted things. The dying birds which Tess comes across are shot by men 'at once so unmannerly and so unchivalrous towards their weaker fellows in Nature's teeming family' (Chapter 41). This and other images of hunting surround Tess's story, along with more subtle images like that of 'the pollard willows, tortured out of their natural shape by incessant choppings' (Chapter 28). In a similar way Hardy supports this view of nature as more fundamental to humanity than the doctrines of society by stressing the way in which the passing seasons actively affect people who are in contact with them. The hiss of fertilisation makes 'the most fanciful bosom grow passionate.' 'The ready bosoms were impregnated by their surroundings.' (Chapter 24). At various times in the book characters feel a sense of oneness with their surroundings, both pleasant and painful. To this extent, then, nature is, in the novel, a 'norm', a standard by which actions and characters can be judged. It is by these standards that Tess's experiences with Alec can be judged a 'liberal education', and the 'social salvation' which could have been achieved by marrying him is to be rejected.

The Trantridge revellers may feel a complete oneness with nature under the influence of drink (Chapter 10), yet at many times in the book we are shown that, though nature may be the most important force in the life of the individual, natural things take scant regard of the happenings which 'cruel Nature's law' has generated. At one time it might be possible to think that worship of the sun was sensible, for 'the luminary was a golden-haired, beaming, mild-eyed, God-like creature, gazing down in the vigour and intentness of youh upon an earth that was brimming with interest for him' (Chapter 14), but when Angel and 'Liza-Lu are walking up the hill to witness Tess's execution 'the sun's rays smiled on pitilessly' (Chapter 59). There are many other examples of the indifference of nature.

Nature, then, may be a better standard than society's artificial rules, but it also forms one of the pressures upon characters, and though they may feel at times a sympathy with it, yet it remains passively indifferent to their sufferings.

The picture Hardy presents of human life is not a cheerful one, but we must not exaggerate his pessimism. Nor must we suggest, because he presents so powerfully the operation of uncontrollable forces upon the individual and the effect of apparently chance happenings, that Hardy has a view of human life in which the conduct of the individual makes little difference to his fate. He is capable of suggesting the vitality of the will to life and joy (particularly in the Talbothays section of the work), of showing real moral growth (especially in the character of Angel Clare), and also, in the character of Tess, of showing how the flawed human being can rise to great dignity in suffering. Whatever the pressures upon her, she is yet to some extent responsible for what happens to her – with greater determination she could have refused to live with Alec, she could have told Angel earlier of her past, she could have found help earlier from Angel's parents. We are made to understand why she did not do these things, and to account for them with subtlety, but this does not obscure her own responsibility for her fate. But as she endures the suffering of Flintcomb-Ash and the degradation she chooses for the sake of her family, she shows a very human, but nonetheless heroic quality.

Structure

When a novelist selects and arranges his material he has two main aims: to make his story convincing and interesting and also to direct the reader's attention directly and indirectly to the main themes and concerns which arise out of the story itself. If the novelist is a scrupulous artist (and Hardy certainly is) then his care will extend to all aspects of the work, and it is therefore best to look at each area separately.

Narrative

Any novel is, of course, selective in its depiction of incident. In *Tess* Hardy highlights and focusses this selectivity by concentrating the narrative into 'phases', each of which is concerned with a key time in Tess's life. What happens in between is lightly sketched, if at all. This ensures that the reader's attention is kept firmly on the story of the heroine, and at the same time enables Hardy to give each episode its individual shape. In any long narrative there are periods of greater and less tension, of reflection and of incident, but by dividing his story in this way Hardy is able to manipulate the feelings of his reader in shorter bursts. The student should examine each phase separately, to see how Hardy places the key moments of action or emotion in such a way as to maintain the interest of the reader. In the first phase, for example, there are two main incidents, the death of the horse, and Tess's seduction, the first a sudden surprise, the second coming with a kind of inevitability. The beginning and end of the phase are linked together, for at the opening we hear of Tess's ancestry, at the end Hardy reflects that 'doubtless some of Tess d'Urbervilles mailed ancestors . . . had dealt the same measure even more ruthlessly towards peasant girls of their time'. This is not just a narrative connection, for Hardy goes on to reflect on the morality of visiting the sins of the fathers on the children – thus raising directly one of the most important themes of the novel, the relationship of one generation to another. Phase the Fourth, by contrast, has comparatively little action; the focus would appear to be Tess's marriage to Angel, but in fact we have been warned by its title 'The Consequence', and by Tess's preoccupation throughout with whether or not to tell Angel of her past, to see that the real focus is whether she will tell, and what his reaction will be. It is therefore dramatic and appropriate that it should end on their wedding night with Tess's confession.

The arrangement of the narrative in this form also allows Hardy very easily to reinforce the reader's reaction to incident by setting it against an appropriate seasonal background. The rhythm of the year, and the relationship of the feelings of characters to seasons, form an important line of continuity in the novel. At least as important is the way unforgettable pictures of the characters against seasonal landscape heighten the emotional response to Tess's fluctuating fortunes. The innocence of the spring opening, the richness of full summer at Talbothays, and the harshness of the winter landscape at Flintcomb-Ash are each both appropriate to Tess's story, and powerful in their supporting of the reader's response to her situation.

Though the division of the novel into phases is its most obvious structural feature, Hardy is careful not to parcel his story up too neatly, for in this, as in all things in a novel which claims to be realistic, there is a narrow line to be followed between random organisation which would be 'natural' but leave no coherent impression, and a tight formal structure in which the hand of the writer is so clear that the realism is impaired. Across the main dividing lines in *Tess* runs the pattern which is made by Tess's successive journeys to and from her home. Her various expeditions are linked to the various stages of her story, but do not coincide exactly. There are four main ones – to Trantridge, to Talbothays, to Flintcomb-Ash, and finally to Sandbourne. Other journeys are introduced – to Emminster, and the final flight which ends at Stonehenge. The main functions of this narrative structure are, first, to emphasise the way Tess is a creature who has her roots in her home and family; second, to provide a means by which the reader can stand back and compare the various stages of her story as she returns, variously affected by experience, to the same point; third, and perhaps the most important, to employ the image of Tess walking various roads to suggest the way in which we are witnessing the spiritual and physical journey which everyone makes along 'the road to dusty death'.

Characters

The individual characteristics of the figures in the novel have already been discussed, but it is vital to realise the ways in which Hardy uses the people he has created in a patterned and organised way.

Tess learns during her life of 'the cruelty of lust and the fragility of love' (Chapter 41), and in the story each side of her suffering is represented by one man. In discussion of the characters of Alec and Angel, and in notes to various chapters, attention has been drawn to the very explicit way Hardy connects these two figures, both by contrasting the ways in which they treat Tess on similar occasions, and by pointing to some similarities in their conduct towards her. Both men, for very different reasons, cause Tess similar suffering. At least as important, however, is the structural function of the comparison. For in dealing with two male figures who affect Tess's life at different times Hardy has the problem that the story requires each of them to be completely absent from the scene for approximately half the book. There is, therefore, a great danger of the narrative falling apart into two distinct stories linked only by the central character. By recalling the actions of one character as the other is placed in a similar situation, Hardy keeps both men present in the reader's mind throughout the book. So, for example, when Angel is driving Tess to the station (Chapter 31) the shadowy figure of Alec driving her to Trantridge is recalled. In the same way, when Alec offers to marry Tess and take her away with him to Africa (Chapter 46), we are explicitly reminded of the man who did marry her and is thinking of taking her to Brazil. The complex network of relationships between the three characters is focussed in the title of Phase the Sixth 'The Convert', for in this section of the book not only is Alec shown as a convert to Christianity, but he is converted again by the ideas of Angel; Angel is converted from his former trust in reason to a recognition of his love for Tess, and Tess herself is converted by Alec from her complete trust in Angel. Thus the parallels between the two male characters help to preserve the coherence of the novel.

For a novel of such length, *Tess* has very few minor characters. Some of their functions have already been outlined, but it remains to add a little about their place in the book's structure. Some critics find the way the farm at Flintcomb-Ash is peopled exclusively by figures from the past strains the believability of the novel. There is some force in this objection, but at the same time Hardy gains a great deal from the concentration. In part it helps to give solidity to figures who might otherwise remain shadowy (in the same way that returning to the figure of the man with the pot of red paint helps to soften the melodrama of his first appearance), but the main effect is to emphasise structurally the way in which the past keeps crowding in upon Tess.

Cross-reference, omens and images

Under this heading are collected a wide range of other devices which Hardy uses to organise and control the reader's reactions to the book.

A fairly straightforward way of linking the various parts of the narrative together is the repetition of similar incidents under different circumstances. Many such repetitions have been mentioned in the discussion of Alec and Angel, but the novel is full of such moments. Two fairly straightforward examples are the very different circumstances under which we see Tess as one of a number of people working on the land – most notably in the comparison of her harvesting at Marlott (Chapter 14), with the swede-hacking and threshing at Flintcomb-Ash (Chapters 43, 47). In each case Tess has managed to overcome a traumatic experience – of the birth of her child, and of the departure of her husband – and to achieve some sort of stability in work. But the similarity only serves to point up the difference between her state then and now, a difference emphasised by the difference of season and work. Another such comparison is the way Tess is dressed up by her mother to go to Trantridge and later Izz and Marian perform the same service before she sets out to Emminster (Chapters 7, 54). The major effect here is to suggest before Tess goes to Emminster that her errand is in some way to be fated, a feeling which is fulfilled when on the way back she meets Alec again. Thus her early and late encounters with him are linked together by a small, but significant narrative recollection. 'Dressing-up', of course, is a motif which extends further through the book; when Angel first sees Tess she is in her finery for the club-walking, on their wedding night she wears jewels, and when he returns she is dressed up, but this time in Alec's extravagant presents.

Such careful links between different parts of the book help to give it a sense of unity, and to sharpen the reader's awareness of how the past and present of the story are brought together.

There are many examples of omens and foreshadowings of one sort and another throughout the book. Some of them, like the afternoon-crowing cock on the day of the wedding, or even the long story of Jack Dollop, seem rather heavy-handed in their creation of a sense of foreboding. All his life Hardy was interested in such country superstitions and omens, and it is perhaps true to suggest that his enthusiasm on occasion ran away with him. But there are many much subtler foreshadowings which do increase the book's power. Their effect, generally, is on the one hand to create an appropriate atmosphere for the narrative that is to come, and on the other, to make the reader feel, when he realises that an event is a fulfillment of something already prefigured, a sense of the inevitability of the story.

One of the subtlest techniques Hardy uses in *Tess* is that of building up various series of connected images. Not content with the careful patterning of events, characters and various explicit foreshadowings, he creates tiny correspondences of image and verbal detail which run like threads throughout the book. These threads work subtly and directly upon the feelings of the reader, conditioning his reactions to events almost without his being aware. There are many such patterns; here are two of them.

When Alec returns to Tess after he has gone to find out where they are he stumbles over her: 'He knelt and bent lower, till her breath warmed his face, and in a moment his cheek was in contact with hers. She was sleeping soundly, and upon her eyelashes there lingered tears.' (Chapter 11). This picture is a striking one, and its pathos is heightened by the tears which Tess has already wept, not knowing how much more she will soon have to weep for. On at least three later occasions this image is recalled. When walking with Angel in the early morning 'Minute diamonds of moisture from the mist hung upon Tess's eyelashes' (Chapter 20). Later, when she avoids telling him the true reason for her hesitancy in marrying him, they are standing in a fog 'settling on the lashes of her eyes, where it rested like crystals' (Chapter 31). Thus in two contexts where Tess and Angel are declaring their love, nature provides an image which recalls the moment just before her first sad encounter with passion. The last image is slightly different, for this time it is Angel who weeps as he smothers his affection for her after her confession: 'a tear descended slowly upon his cheek, a tear so large that it magnified the pores of the skin over which it rolled, like the object lens of a microscope.' (Chapter 35). Here, for a moment, Angel's true feelings emerge, though Tess 'hardly observed' this minutely described tear. Hardy creates a complex set of feelings in the reader, for he sees very clearly what Angel is suppressing and Tess not noticing, and, with the memory of Tess's tears before her rape, and its later recollection, feels its poignancy more than either.

Another pattern of imagery is that which associates fog and mist with passion and sexuality. When Tess is raped it is foggy; when she first approaches Angel as he is playing the harp she passes through 'juicy grass which sent up mists of pollen' (Chapter 19); much of their courtship takes place in misty mornings and evenings. Before all these, in the description of the dancers at Chaseborough, there is an explicit link made between the mist of dust and pollen which obscures them from view, and its ability to transform them into lustful classical demi-gods – a transformation which vanishes when they come out into the clear evening air. It is difficult to pin suggestive images like these down to a single significance, but it seems clear enough that Hardy is linking passion both with the natural world, and also with concealment and confusion. When the reader meets images of fog and mist associated with Tess and Angel he is reminded very explicitly of the dangers and excess of passion and lust. Thus even images in themselves attractive are contaminated by the network of associations built up round them.

There are many other such chains of imagery running through the book. The student should consider, for example, the way in which the colour white is linked with innocence, red with passion, with blood and misfortune; or the various images derived from the biblical account of the Garden of Eden, the Paradise in which man first sinned; or the malevolent associations built up round descriptions of fire.

The whole of this section emphasises the care over detail which Hardy shows in his control of various kinds of structure in *Tess*. Such care is especially appropriate in a book which is concerned very specifically with 'the mesh of events' in the life of its heroine. As he recognises the intricate mesh which Hardy creates the reader is experiencing himself the artistic equivalent of the 'real' mesh which entraps Tess.

Narrative technique

Even if a novelist bases individual incidents on things from his own experience or from history he is responsible for the selection and arrangement of the material. But the writer has a wide range of possible ways to present his story. He can present it as if he were recording something that actually happened (in which case he cannot claim too great an insight into what his characters are thinking), or he can make no effort to disguise the fact that the people and events are his creation, and therefore feel free to inform the reader about the motivation and thoughts of people in a way impossible in real life. Other alternatives are to present the story as if it were an autobiography, or to present it consistently from the viewpoint of one of the characters within the story. There are many other possibilities which need not concern us. In recent years it has become customary for novelists (and critics) to worry a great deal about telling a story from some consistent standpoint, or 'point of view'. Though Hardy was not much concerned with consistency – at different times he writes from various points of view – the reader should try to understand and to distinguish the different techniques Hardy employs.

When Angel joins the club-walking dance, he chooses a partner, but, we are told, 'The name of the eclipsing girl, whatever it was, has not been handed down' (Chapter 2). This seems to imply that Hardy is retelling a familiar story, which just happens to be deficient in a few details. Rather the same standpoint is implied when he describes the house where Tess and Angel spend their wedding-night: its 'exterior features are so well known to all travellers' (Chapter 34). Of course, most of the places in Hardy's novels are based on real Dorset towns, and Hardy is here doing no more than remind the reader of the solid authenticity of his settings. In a more surprising way, Hardy once adopts this stance in relation to his heroine, when he speaks of 'the stopt-diapason note which her voice acquired when her heart was in her speech, and *which will never be forgotten by those who knew her*' (Chapter 14). Oddly, this remark, which should serve to distance the narrator from his story, actually suggests the passionate commitment Hardy has to his heroine, so vividly does she live in his imagination.

Something of the same stance is suggested, more indirectly, by the way Hardy records that Angel and Tess's despairing walk on their wedding-night was seen by a cottager, who remembered the incident a long time later (Chapter 35). Here it is as if the novelist is reporting an incident handed down in local history, though the dominant picture is of a scene overlooked by a figure who has little direct interest in it.

Presenting parts of the narrative as they are seen by the eyes of characters within the novel is a manner of which Hardy was very fond. The two most obvious examples are the caretaker of the untenanted house in which Angel and Tess camp (Chapter 58), and, even more strikingly, Alec's landlady, Mrs Brooks (Chapter 56), but numerous other briefer examples could be found elsewhere in the novel. The effect of this technique is at once to bring the reader close to the events being described, and yet at the same time to detach him from the intricacies of feeling which might be involved, for these onlookers have no direct concern with what they see. We thus get pictures of great precision and clarity in which the scene as a whole makes an impact.

Related to this technique, but rather different in effect, is the presentation of incidents and scenes through the eyes of the main characters. For example, in Chapter 27 Tess is described as she is seen through Angel's eyes. This is both appropriate and effective, for Angel has been away telling his parents of his wish to marry Tess, and so the detailed description fits his heightened emotion as he returns to Talbothays. In a similar way the contrast between the outdoor freshness of the club-walking and the squalor of the Durbeyfield household is rendered more dramatic by its presentations through the eyes and ears of Tess as she approaches her home (Chapter 3). This technique is used most often, as is only to be expected, in creating a sense of involvement with Tess, and nowhere to greater effect than in the description of her night-time journey home to her sick mother in Chapter 50, where the vividness of her imagination under emotional strain is captured, as well as the complex emotions she feels on seeing her home again.

In contrast to the presentation of incidents as seen by detached observers, the technique here involves the reader in a more complex fashion, for he is both responding to the dramatic immediateness and also becoming directly involved in the emotions and reactions of characters.

At other times in the book Hardy himself adopts as narrator a detached stance, as if he were describing a scene vividly before his eyes, but without any special access to the minds of the human beings who people the landscape. This is particularly true of his descriptions of place, or of groups of people at work, and is shown at its very best in the long prelude to Chapter 14. In this section he gradually narrows the description down until 'the eye returns involuntarily to the girl in the pink cotton jacket'. The reader suspects that this girl is Tess, but this is not confirmed for some time; it is as if Hardy wishes to stress not her individuality, but her community with the whole agricultural and peasant world.

Hardy frequently, of course, does present in his own voice reactions to scenes, character's thoughts and the like. Generally he does so in an unforced and convincing manner, but there are a few occasions when the reader feels that he is distorting the scene to make a propaganda point. This is often true when he is talking about religious observance. Hardy himself was not a believer, and he seems to have found it inconceivable that anyone else could have been sincere. Or else he is inclined at times to present a character's thoughts in language that is too sophisticated to be convincing (see for example Mrs Durbeyfield's thoughts as expressed in Chapter 3). Finally, on a very few occasions, Hardy's temptation to preach to his readers overcomes his tact, and he labours his reflections. Examples might be the section on the Durbeyfield children (Chapter 4), where the misery of their plight is quite well enough established without the moralising, or the long paragraph at the end of the next chapter, where Hardy leaps into speculative philosophy when all he really wants to say is that it was a pity that Tess met Alec.

Despite these occasional blemishes, Hardy generally handles his different narrative perspectives with some skill, and it is worth the student's while to ask himself continually 'through whose eyes is this scene presented?', and then to try to suggest why a particular viewpoint is chosen at a particular time, and what effects Hardy gains from his choice.

Style

In conventional terms, Hardy does not have a 'good' style – he tends to use long words where shorter ones would be more direct and effective; his sentences are often clumsily put together. At one time in his life he made a deliberate attempt to 'improve' his style by a course of reading in approved authors. It is not difficult to find passages where clumsy pomposity gets in the way of what he is trying to say. One example might be this sentence: 'Verily another girl than the simple one she had been at home was she who, bowed by thought, stood still here, and turned to look behind her.' (Chapter 12). The biblical and archaic 'verily' is unconvincing in the context, and the twisted order of ideas in the sentence adds nothing except confusion. Another such is the description of Tess after Angel has left her in the fields: 'When he was gone she stood awhile, thoughtfully peeling the last bud; and then, awakening from her reverie, flung it and all the crowd of floral nobility impatiently on the ground, in añ ebullition of displeasure with herself for her *niaiseries*, and with a quickening warmth in her heart of hearts.' (Chapter 19). A promising scene, expressing Tess's mixed feelings after her conversation with Angel, is completely wrecked by first the unnecessary literariness of the phrase 'floral nobility', and then the impossibly pompous expression of her anger. If Tess's feelings are being expressed, then she would certainly not use the foreign word, and would feel an *anger* with herself, not an 'ebullition of displeasure'.

But though such poor writing can be found, it is quite wrong to dismiss Hardy's style in general, for the test is not whether a style is 'good' in the abstract, but whether it works in its particular context. So, at times, even Hardy's tendency to use unfamiliar words and complex sentences is perfectly appropriate to his purpose. When, for example, he is describing the threshing machine the unfamiliar words emphasise the alien quality of the machine and its operator. Even the peculiar 'autochthonous' – a very rare word – is much more effective than the simple 'native' would be.

In many of his descriptions the loose construction of the sentences helps to give an immediacy and vividness as it induces the eye of the reader to follow the eye of the narrator. When, for example, Angel and Tess sit down, on their wedding night:

Imagination might have beheld a Last Day luridness in this red-coaled glow, which fell on his face and hand, and on hers, peering into the loose hair about her brow, and firing the delicate skin underneath. A large shadow of her shape rose upon the wall and ceiling. She bent forward, at which each diamond on her neck gave a sinister wink like a toad's. (Chapter 34)

It is not only the suggestion of the day of doom which makes this such a powerful passage. For in the structure of the first sentence, with its succession of clauses linked by 'and' we seem to be following the eye of the narrator as it travels across the figures sitting before the fire and onto their shadows. Moreover, it seems almost that the fire itself is animate, as it is 'peering' at the figures. The malevolent atmosphere is further enhanced by the bringing together of 'diamond' and 'toad', with the familiar word 'wink'. The student will find many examples of this sort scattered throughout the work, where the scene is animated as things are given human attributes.

Hardy is also capable of presenting scenes with great simplicity. His description of Tess and Marian at work in the swede-field generates a great deal of its force by the directness of sentences like these: 'In the afternoon the rain came on again, and Marian said that they need not work any more. But if they did not work they would not be paid; so they worked on.' The repetitive quality of the sentences emphasises the lack of choice – they work or starve; the plainness sets out their plight with stark clarity.

In his handling of speech Hardy is variable. Much of the dialect speech is masterly, and a good example to examine in detail is Dairyman Crick's telling of the story of William Dewy (Chapter 17). We seem to hear the natural rhythms of speech in these loosely connected sentences, in the digressions, and, of course, in the use of dialect words and phrases. Elsewhere he can present convincing, immediate dialogue, particularly when it is direct and simple, but too often when people are speaking under the stress of emotion he goes for a heightened, melodramatic manner which does not really ring true. Compare these two exchanges:

'What have I done – what *have* I done! I have not told of anything that interferes with or belies my love for you. You don't think I planned it do you? It is in your own mind what you are angry at, Angel; it is not in me. O it is not in me, and I am not that deceitful woman you think me!'

'H'm well. Not deceitful, my wife; but not the same. No not the same. But do not make me reproach you. I have sworn that I will not; and I will do everything to avoid it.' (Chapter 35)

Here, though everything that is said is perfectly appropriate to the situation, the sentences in Tess's speech are far too neat to be the language of disordered feeling, and though Angel is supposed to be controlling his feelings, he speaks more like a man discussing a philosophical question than someone desperately suppressing conflicting passions. Quite different is the next example:

'Tess! Say it is not true! No, it is not true!'
'It is true.'
'Every word?'
'Every word.'
He looked at her imploringly . . . However she only repeated –
'It is true.'
'Is he living?' Angel then asked.
'The baby died.'
'But the man?'
'He is alive.' (Chapter 36)

Here the interpretation of what is said is confined to the narrator's comments in the middle of the dialogue. The baldness of the question and answer form implies with great power the state of mind of the two characters; Angel's desperate search for a way out frustrated by answers to questions which only confirm his despair, and, on the other side, Tess's fatalistic endurance. The repetition of the opening part of the dialogue also helps to build up in the reader a sense of the inexorable pressure on the characters.

It is not, of course, being suggested that only short, snappy dialogue can be convincing. In Chapter 19, for example, Tess and Angel talk at cross-purposes with one another, and there Hardy is able to convey both Angel's sense of the nature of things, and his fluency in speech as contrasted with Tess's less articulate groping after words to explain how she feels. It is simply that at this particular point in the story Hardy manages to capture the tense emotional situation much better in the terse exchange than in the rather longer set speeches of the first dialogue.

In short, it can be said that Hardy's style is not flawless, but his successes in finding appropriate expression for most of the novel easily outweigh the failures.

Part 4

Hints for study

Reading

Ideally the student should make his first reading of the novel fairly rapid, gaining an idea of the outline of the book, allowing it to work uninterruptedly on his mind and emotions. After all, this is how Hardy wrote the novel to be read, and attempting too early to take notes and to 'make sense' of the book not only deadens the vital first impressions, but makes it impossible to appreciate the large-scale sweep of the novel as a whole. The enormous power of the ending is only fully realised on such an uninterrupted reading. (It is, incidentally, no bad plan if the student rereads the whole book in this sort of way in the days immediately before an examination.)

On his second reading the student should take a chapter at a time, consulting the glossary in Part 2 of these Notes, making sure that he has understood what Hardy is saying. He might also consider some of the notes provided before each glossary, and begin to get a sense of the way each chapter works dramatically.

If circumstances allow, it should not be until after this second reading is completed that the student reads the critical section of this guide, or follows up some of the suggestions for further reading given in Part 5. Reading criticism too soon can be misleading, for the student is likely to see in the book only what other people tell him he should see, rather than using criticism to help him to express what *he* sees in the book, or to deepen his own understanding. It cannot be stressed too often that the student must always test what others say about the book against his own experience of reading it.

It is on the third reading, after consultation of some critical works, that the student should start to take detailed notes. The purpose of note-taking is twofold:

(a) to concentrate the reader's mind on formulating precisely what Hardy is getting at, and his own detailed response to the text;

(b) To build up a body of references which will act as an aid to the memory, and will be helpful in reminding the reader of significant aspects of the book when writing essays.

Notes should, therefore, be taken in a form which will allow for their easy consultation and use. So too, they should be full enough to ensure that they make sense when read over at a later date, but not so copious that it would be easier to reread the whole novel. A sensible way of satisfying these various requirements is to prepare, before the reading of the novel, a number of sheets of notepaper each with a separate heading covering one of the key aspects of the novel. The student could use as a guide the various headings in the critical section of this study, though dividing up the section entitled 'themes' into various sub-headings – 'past and present'; 'nature'; 'conflict of natural and conventional values' and so on, and perhaps also dividing the section on style into headings such as 'description'; 'narrative'; 'dialogue'. Then, as the reading proceeds, the student can jot down quotations particularly relevant to one or other aspect of the book on the appropriate sheet of paper. Remember to put the page reference with each quotation so that it can be found again easily. These notes should not only include quotations, but should also provide a record of the reader's reaction to certain passages, otherwise, when consulted later, they will mean very little. (It is also possible to take notes from critics in the same sort of way, adding to the information on specific subjects, rather than taking general and unsorted notes.) Remember these points when taking notes:

(1) Be *selective*. Write down only references to passages which strike you as especially important, otherwise the notes will be confusing rather than helpful.

(2) It is very tempting just to write down the comments that Hardy makes in his own voice in the novel; at least as telling are quotations which demonstrate how his comments are put into practice. For example: the reader will certainly want to note down on the sheet devoted to Tess Hardy's comment on the language Tess uses, perhaps in this form:

> p.48 (Chapter 3) Tess, because of her education 'spoke two languages; the dialect at home, more or less; ordinary English abroad and to persons of quality.'

But it would be as useful to note:

> p.300 (Chapter 37) Tess uses dialect form when she returns home: 'I don't know how to *tell 'ee*, mother.'

(3) Some passages will figure on more than one sheet. For example: Under the heading of Angel Clare's character might be a note:

> p.227 (Chapter 30) Angel shows consideration to Tess on drive to station.

But on the sheet devoted to structure (perhaps under a sub-heading 'Characters') the same reference would be given, in this sort of form:

Chapter 30 Angel shows a very different attitude to Tess from that shown by Alec in the earlier drive to Trantridge.

(Notice, by the way, that it is not always necessary to write down a specific quotation, when it is the general outline of an episode which is important.)

When the notes are completed it will probably be necessary to do some further sorting into smaller sub-headings, and to sift out some of the less important or merely repetitive references. The student is then equipped with a handy guide to the novel, in a form which makes it easier to assemble relevant material for essays, and suitable for last-minute refreshing of the memory before an examination. Furthermore, notes built up in this kind of way are much easier to add to, both on subsequent rereadings of the novel, and after reading critics.

Writing

There are a few general rules which should be followed in writing any essay.

(1) Take time to think about the question before starting to write. It is obviously essential to answer the question which is being asked precisely and directly. Especially in examinations it is very easy to seize on a part of the question which seems familiar and to rush into writing, only to find half-way through that you are not answering the question at all.

(2) Select relevant material. In a novel as long as *Tess* a great deal happens, and it is vital before beginning to write to select those sections and aspects of the book which are relevant to the particular question, ignoring marginal or irrelevant matter. For example, if a question reads: 'How far is Tess responsible for her own suffering?' then the student should think of various episodes when this question is uppermost, such as the episodes of her seduction, of her marriage and confession, of Flintcomb-Ash, of rejoining, then murdering Alec. Each episode will then be assessed independently, asking in each case how far Tess's own conduct determined the outcome. There may be other episodes which could be relevant – such as the death of the horse, Prince, which starts the process of Tess's suffering, or the death of her baby, Sorrow. But not everything can be included, and the most important must be preferred.

(3) Plan the arrangement of the chosen material:
(*a*) *Introduction.* In answering the question about Tess's responsibility for her own suffering it would obviously be wrong to begin with an introduction like this: 'When the story opens, Tess, a sixteen-year-old girl, is living with her parents in the village of Marlott.' For, though this

sentence contains information which might be relevant to the question – her youth makes her easier prey for Alec, and the influence of her parents is presented by Hardy as one of the influences which shape Tess's life – it does not attack the question directly. A better beginning would be something like this:

> 'During her brief life Tess endures a great deal of suffering which comes about as a result of the actions of other people over whom she has no control, or as a result of the operation of chance. Moreover, Hardy stresses that she has equally little responsibility for many aspects of her character, which are moulded by the influences of people, place and history. Yet at many of the key points in the novel Tess herself could have changed the course of events.'

Here there is a clear, direct response to the particular question, and an approach to the answer is firmly indicated.

(b) *The body of the essay.* It would be very easy to answer this question by recounting in the order in which they appear in the book the various events in Tess's life, delivering a verdict on the degree of her responsibility as each is dealt with. This approach would not be fatal, but it would be far better to consider a different sort of organisation. In the sample introduction it has been suggested that there are two sides to the case – on the one hand Tess is very much the victim of various circumstances, but on the other she does have some responsibility for what happens to her. It is better, then, to make the structure of the essay follow the structure of the *argument*, rather than the order of the narrative.

The student should therefore list first the factors over which she has no control:

(i) Her family's misfortunes, both at the beginning and the end of the book.

(ii) The characters of the two men in her life, for both Alec and Angel cause her suffering.

(iii) The operation of chance, as in the death of Prince, or the failure of her letter to be seen by Clare.

(iv) The pressure of social convention which decrees that what happened to her at Trantridge was sinful – shown both early in the book, and in the pressure that forces the family to leave home after Jack's death.

(v) The inheritance of various qualities from her family.

(vi) Hardy's view of the inevitability of 'flux and reflux'; of the operation of an inevitable pattern of rise and fall in human life.

This is not a complete list, but some such collection should be made. Then on the other side should be listed the various ways in which Tess does have real choice, and exercises it in a fashion which increases her suffering.

>   (*i*) Her readiness to submit to the wishes and opinions of others – to Alec, in living with him after the rape; to Angel in accepting entirely his view of their situation.
>
>   (*ii*) Her pride, which prevents her from telling her parents the true state of affairs.
>
>   (*iii*) Her continual putting off of the decision to tell Angel the story of her past – a kind of cowardice.
>
>   (*iv*) The fact that she ultimately commits a crime to gain her freedom.

After lists such as these have been made, then the body of the essay can be planned to show first one side of the case, and then the other.

(4) Choose the evidence to support the argument. So far we have mainly been concerned with *what* is said or shown in the novel. At least as important is to show *how* it is said. So, for example, when discussing the pressure of social convention on Tess, the point can be clinched by quoting Hardy's comment 'most of the misery had been generated by her conventional aspect' (Chapter 14). Her total submissiveness to Angel could be aptly illustrated by a quotation such as Tess's words 'I will obey you like your wretched slave, even if it is to lie down and die.' (Chapter 35). The amount of quotation, and the detail with which it is analysed will vary according to the nature of the question and the circumstances under which the essay is being written. So, for example, if the question is 'Show how Hardy uses description to reinforce the reader's sense of Tess's misfortunes', then the student would take a passage like the description of turnip hacking at Flintcomb-Ash (Chapter 43), and subject it to close analysis, showing how Hardy increases the sense of the active hostility of nature by describing field and sky as having human, though featureless faces; how the toil of the work is conveyed by the mechanical language of 'the business of the two women was to grub up the lower or earthy half of the root with a hooked fork called a hacker'; how the reader's attention is concentrated by the observation of tiny detail of the girls' dress.

When essays are being written as part of the process of studying a book such quotation and analysis should be extensive and detailed – apart from anything else, it makes the essays more valuable for revision – but under examination conditions long quotations are neither possible nor desirable unless the student has an unusually accurate and retentive memory. Far too often the amount of time spent in learning long quotations only means that examination answers are slanted to allow the student to make use of his available quotations, whether they are strictly relevant or not, and the time spent in recalling the material and the anxiety about whether it has been remembered accurately prevent the student from getting on with the planning and writing of the essay itself. It is far better, when dealing with a long prose work, to concentrate on remembering a substantial number of *short* quotations, and in examination essays to give precise references to an episode rather than attempting to quote Hardy's exact words.

(5) When the main part of the essay has been written, the student should aim at a firm, short conclusion, which summarises the argument and leaves the reader with a clear sense of what the essay has demonstrated. So, for example, in concluding the essay on Tess's responsibility for her suffering we might say:

'The tone of the concluding paragraph of Tess's story indicates clearly that Hardy considered that she had been the plaything of a careless universe, and, as we have seen, the pressure of various kinds upon Tess is extremely powerful. Nonetheless, however we may account for her conduct, it is clear that at several points in her story she could have chosen a different course from that she actually pursued, and so she must bear part of the responsibility for her suffering. Indeed, it is this element of human choice which makes her tragedy so powerful, and ensures the reader's deep emotional involvement with her plight.'

All that has been said in this section can be summed up briefly:

Select the material appropriate to the question.
Organise it in the way which best supports the argument.
Support it with relevant, precisely indicated evidence from the text.
Introduce and conclude the argument clearly and succinctly.

(Notice that the introduction and conclusion are placed last in this list. It is often better to think about the body of the essay first, as this helps to clarify the line of your argument, rather than plunging into an introduction which then proves inadequate for the material which is subsequently used.)

Revision

If notes have been taken in the way suggested in the section on 'reading' then they should be in a suitable form for rereading in the last few days before an examination. It is a good idea to go through them, selecting the most important points, the most useful short quotations, and then to write these key things down on a fresh piece of paper, so that you have a concentrated version available for last-minute revision. The process of selection is itself a valuable aid to revision, since it forces the student to think about what really matters in the novel.

The student should check that he is quite sure of exactly what happens, and in what order events occur. Under the pressure of examination it is easy to lose confidence, and to find oneself wondering if, for example, Tess meets Alec again before or after she visits Angel's parents, before or after her father dies, and whether the meeting takes place in the fifth or sixth phase of the book. The best thing to do is to read quickly through the summaries in these Notes, and then to try to write down, from memory, the chief events in each phase of the book.

One of the greatest dangers in preparing for an examination is that the process of distillation, selection, and memorising, tends to make the book itself become rather remote. A complete, quick re-reading of the whole novel will restore some of the freshness of response to essays. It is worth remembering always that literary criticism is basically a way of explaining how and why a book affects each individual reader, and essays which convey to the reader some sense of the student's own response to the work, his enthusiasm and enjoyment of what he has read, are much more pleasurable than those which seem only to reflect the toil and hard work of trying to say the 'right' things.

Questions

The questions which follow are roughly grouped by subject. In each section the easier questions come first.

Characters

---

(1) How far, and in what ways, is the character of Tess influenced by her parents?

Chapter 3 contains some of the most extended treatment of the subject; Tess considers the matter herself in Chapter 16. Numerous comments are scattered through the book. Also to be considered is the way her mother's lack of warning about 'men-folk' is thought by both Tess (Chapter 12) and Alec (Chapter 46) to have been blameworthy. Her parent's wish for a successful match pushes her towards Alec, and influences her decision not to tell Angel her past.

(2) Does Hardy manage to make us sympathise with Angel's rejection of Tess?

Here the student must consider three rather different things:

(*i*) Is Angel made out to be in any way a sympathetic character? – consideration might be given to his courteousness to Tess and the others at Talbothays.

(*ii*) Does Hardy give us enough evidence to understand why he behaves as he does? – consult Part 3 of these Notes.

(*iii*) At the actual critical moment when Angel rejects Tess, does Hardy allow us to see clearly enough into Angel's feelings so that, even if we do not like what he does, we can sympathise with the struggle? – the sleep-walking scene is significant here.

(3) 'Whatever Alec d'Urberville does, Hardy never succeeds in making us believe in him as anything but a stage villain.' Discuss.

When a question is put in this form, then the answer has to take into account all the implications of the quotation. Therefore there are a number of different ways of approaching the question:

(*i*) Picking especially on the last phrase of the quotation, 'a stage villain', you might want to argue that at various times Alec is not villainous at all; he appears to care genuinely for Tess, he is generous to her family, even if his motives are suspect.

(*ii*) The phrase 'whatever he does' clearly indicates that the answer to the question must face the problem of the various characters Alec assumes during the book. You might want to argue that, though you find the conversion unconvincing, you find the depiction of him as a 'horsey young buck' quite real.

(*iii*) Part of the question is obviously aimed at the way Hardy presents the character, through action and through dialogue. You should therefore say whether you find these aspects of Alec convincing or not – perhaps by close analysis of a single scene in which he is involved.

(4) How do the comparisons Hardy makes between Tess and the animal world help us to realise the nature of her tragedy?

(5) 'Tess shows a great deal of courage in the book; but courage and pride are closely linked, and we might think that she would have done better to be more of a coward.' Discuss.

(6) Show how Angel Clare matures as a man during the book.

(7) In the course of writing the novel Hardy changed the name of Tess's seducer from 'Hawnferne' to 'd'Urberville'; what effects did he gain from this decision?

(8) What would *Tess of the d'Urbervilles* lose if the characters of Marian, Retty and Izz were simply omitted from the book?

(9) 'We cannot admire Tess's parents, but we can and do feel pity for them.' Do you agree?

(10) The comment Hardy makes about Tess, that 'most of the misery had been generated by her conventional aspect', is at least as true of Angel. Discuss the ways in which both characters struggle with their inherited values.

When discussing questions which take in more than one character, it is sensible to keep a proper balance between the two. When planning the essay, try not to deal first with one and then the other, but to compare and contrast throughout.

(11) What problems does Hardy have in developing the characters of Alec and Angel, because each is only present for half the book, and with what success does he solve them?

(12) Hardy wrote: 'I am convinced that persons are successively various persons, according as each special strand in their characters is brought uppermost by circumstances.' Show how the various circumstances in which the characters in *Tess* are placed emphasise different aspects of their characters.

Themes

(1) How does Hardy convey to the reader the sense of the presence of the past in the present?

Various aspects of this subject should be separated:

(*i*) The way hardy describes places in terms of their history, for example Chapter 2, Chapter 9.

(*ii*) The ever-present motif of the d'Urberville family, for example Chapter 1, Chapter 11, Chapter 52. Some effort should be made to classify the many references according to their context.

(*iii*) The way characters from the past recur in the story, for example Farmer Groby.

Other things could be added to this list. Notice that the question is about Hardy's *way* of presenting the theme, so it is not enough to say that 'the presence of the past in the present is important' – you must construct an answer on an exploration of the different methods.

(2) Show how Hardy creates in the reader a sense of the oppressiveness of conventional social values.

The main examples will obviously be Angel and Tess, but the student should resist the temptation to write a character study, and should concentrate on the way in which the weight of these values is conveyed, for example in Chapter 13.

The student should also consider other ways in which the awareness of the *nature* of these values is created, for example through the characters of Angel's family, especially his brothers, or the hypocritical villagers who disapprove of Tess's conduct.

(3) Explore the implications of the phrase 'Cruel Nature's law', and show how the destructive aspect of Nature influences events in the novel.

(4) Tess suffers, says Hardy, from 'the cruelty of lust and the fragility of love'. Show how the reader's sense of the cruelty and fragility is built up.

Again, this is a question which focusses the student's attention on two characters, Alec and Angel, but does not ask simply for a character study. The student should consider the way Alec's conduct continually demonstrates his desire for 'mastery', and the way he is associated in the latter stages of the book with the harsh, impersonal machinery of Flintcomb-Ash. Similarly he should look at the various ways in which the happiness of the time at Talbothays is continually undermined, the ways in which it is made clear that Angel's love for Tess is dangerously unphysical.

Structure

(1) Show how Hardy keeps the reader's interest from phase to phase.

(2) Examine Phase the First carefully, showing how Hardy sets in motion the action of the book, and also prepares the way for some of the novel's main themes.

(3) Why do you think Hardy begins the book with Jack's meeting with Parson Tringham, rather than with the club-walking?

(4) Examine carefully any chapter of the book, showing how Hardy uses the alternation of dialogue, action and description to build up a feeling of suspense in the reader.

Good examples might be Chapter 4; Chapter 14; Chapter 30; Chapter 34; Chapter 58.

(5) What is the importance to the novel's thematic content of the structural motif of Tess's repeated returns to her home?

This is quite a complicated question. A sensible procedure would be to look first at the various scenes of homecoming in Chapters 12, 38, 50, paying special attention to what Hardy tells us about Tess's feelings. Then the student should consider what the consequences of the returns are in each case. Normally home is a place of security and rest, but for Tess it is a place of care and distress. Finally an attempt might be made to consider the ways in which these episodes highlight the family's responsibility for Tess's misfortunes, and intensify the d'Urberville motif.

(6) Demonstrate the various ways in which Hardy prepares the reader for events that are to come later.

See the section on the subject in the critical section. Distinguish carefully between different kinds of foreshadowing.

Style and narrative

(1) Contrast the descriptions of Flintcomb-Ash and Talbothays, showing how Hardy creates a sense of a world appropriate to the stages in Tess's story.

(2) Does the plot of *Tess* rely too much upon chance coincidences to be believable?

(3) 'Some of the scenes in *Tess* which are most improbable are the most imaginatively effective.' Discuss.

Examples might be the meeting with the man with the red paint in Chapter 12, or Angel's sleepwalking in Chapter 37.

(4) What kinds of effects does Hardy gain from his use of dialect speech?

Consideration should be given to Tess's parents; to Dairyman Crick and the other milkmaids. It might be argued that there are two almost opposite effects, one suggesting a boorish unlearnedness in the case of the Durbeyfields, the other a straightforward honesty in the case of the characters at Talbothays.

(5) 'Some of the strongest effects in *Tess* are obtained by Hardy's habit of giving human attributes to inanimate things.' Discuss.

There are a whole host of different examples which might be found, for example the description of the wind in Chapter 4, of the fire in Chapter 34, night in Chapter 35, landscape in Chapter 43, machinery in Chapter 47.

(6) Discuss Hardy's successes and failures in creating convincing speech for his characters.

(7) 'When Hardy describes a scene he does not just give his reader a photograph of a place, but creates a mood and set of attitudes at the same time.' Show what techniques Hardy uses to achieve this effect.

(8) Explore the various ways in which Hardy presents scenes and episodes through the eyes of a character within the story, and comment on the effectiveness of the technique.

Part 5

Suggestions for further reading

The text

The best edition is that in Macmillan's New Wessex Editions, General Editor, P. N. Furbank, Macmillan, London, 1974.

Hardy's life

The main source of information for Hardy's life is still the book presented as written by his second wife, but in fact largely written by Hardy himself:

HARDY, F. E.: *The Life of Thomas Hardy*, Macmillan, London, 1962. This collects the two volumes of 1928 and 1930 into one.

Of other books devoted to Hardy's life the best, by a long way, are:

GITTINGS, ROBERT: *Young Thomas Hardy*, Heinemann, London, 1975 and, by the same author, *Older Hardy*, Heinemann, London, 1978.

General reading

Useful studies of the novel are:

HUGMAN, BRUCE: *Hardy: Tess of the d'Urbervilles*, Studies in English Literature No. 43, Edward Arnold, London, 1970.

PINION, F. B.: *A Hardy Companion*, Macmillan, London, 1968. Gives a mass of information about all aspects of Hardy's work and thought.

Studies aimed specifically at introducing Hardy's work are:

SCOTT-JAMES, R. A. and LEWIS, C. DAY: *Thomas Hardy*, Writers and Their Work, Longman, London, 1965.

BUTLER, L. ST.J.: *Thomas Hardy*, Cambridge University Press, Cambridge, 1977.

WILLIAMS, MERRYN: *A Preface to Hardy*, Preface Books, London, 1976.

Many critical works on Thomas Hardy have been published, and the student who wishes to go further should consult the more detailed bibliographies contained in these studies.

The author of these notes

DAVID LINDLEY was educated at Pembroke College, Oxford. After holding a post as Lecturer at Lincoln College, Oxford, he became, in 1973, Lecturer in English Studies at the University of Stirling, moving in 1978 to a lectureship in English Literature at the University of Leeds. An enthusiasm for music, as a performer and conductor, is reflected in his research which is concerned with the relationship of music and poetry in the Renaissance. He is at present engaged in writing a study of the poet-musician Thomas Campion.

York Notes: list of titles

HENRY FIELDING
Joseph Andrews
Tom Jones

F. SCOTT FITZGERALD
Tender is the Night
The Great Gatsby

E. M. FORSTER
A Passage to India
Howards End

ATHOL FUGARD
Selected Plays

JOHN GALSWORTHY
Strife

MRS GASKELL
North and South

WILLIAM GOLDING
Lord of the Flies
The Inheritors
The Spire

OLIVER GOLDSMITH
She Stoops to Conquer
The Vicar of Wakefield

ROBERT GRAVES
Goodbye to All That

GRAHAM GREENE
Brighton Rock
The Heart of the Matter
The Power and the Glory

THOMAS HARDY
Far from the Madding Crowd
Jude the Obscure
Selected Poems
Tess of the D'Urbervilles
The Mayor of Casterbridge
The Return of the Native
The Trumpet Major
The Woodlanders
Under the Greenwood Tree

L. P. HARTLEY
The Go-Between
The Shrimp and the Anemone

NATHANIEL HAWTHORNE
The Scarlet Letter

SEAMUS HEANEY
Selected Poems

ERNEST HEMINGWAY
A Farewell to Arms
For Whom the Bell Tolls
The African Stories
The Old Man and the Sea

GEORGE HERBERT
Selected Poems

HERMANN HESSE
Steppenwolf

BARRY HINES
Kes

HOMER
The Iliad

ANTHONY HOPE
The Prisoner of Zenda

GERARD MANLEY HOPKINS
Selected Poems

WILLIAM DEAN HOWELLS
The Rise of Silas Lapham

RICHARD HUGHES
A High Wind in Jamaica

THOMAS HUGHES
Tom Brown's Schooldays

ALDOUS HUXLEY
Brave New World

HENRIK IBSEN
A Doll's House
Ghosts
Hedda Gabler

HENRY JAMES
Daisy Miller
The Europeans
The Portrait of a Lady
The Turn of the Screw
Washington Square

SAMUEL JOHNSON
Rasselas

BEN JONSON
The Alchemist
Volpone

JAMES JOYCE
A Portrait of the Artist as a Young Man
Dubliners

JOHN KEATS
Selected Poems

RUDYARD KIPLING
Kim

D. H. LAWRENCE
Sons and Lovers
The Rainbow
Women in Love

CAMARA LAYE
L'Enfant Noir

HARPER LEE
To Kill a Mocking-Bird

LAURIE LEE
Cider with Rosie

THOMAS MANN
Tonio Kröger

CHRISTOPHER MARLOWE
Doctor Faustus
Edward II

ANDREW MARVELL
Selected Poems

W. SOMERSET MAUGHAM
Of Human Bondage
Selected Short Stories

J. MEADE FALKNER
Moonfleet

HERMAN MELVILLE
Billy Budd
Moby Dick

THOMAS MIDDLETON
Women Beware Women

THOMAS MIDDLETON *and* WILLIAM ROWLEY
The Changeling

ARTHUR MILLER
Death of a Salesman
The Crucible

JOHN MILTON
Paradise Lost I & II
Paradise Lost IV & IX
Selected Poems

V. S. NAIPAUL
A House for Mr Biswas

SEAN O'CASEY
Juno and the Paycock
The Shadow of a Gunman

GABRIEL OKARA
The Voice

EUGENE O'NEILL
Mourning Becomes Electra

GEORGE ORWELL
Animal Farm
Nineteen Eighty-four

JOHN OSBORNE
Look Back in Anger

WILFRED OWEN
Selected Poems

ALAN PATON
Cry, The Beloved Country

THOMAS LOVE PEACOCK
Nightmare Abbey and *Crotchet Castle*

HAROLD PINTER
The Birthday Party
The Caretaker

PLATO
The Republic

ALEXANDER POPE
Selected Poems

THOMAS PYNCHON
The Crying of Lot 49

SIR WALTER SCOTT
Ivanhoe
Quentin Durward
The Heart of Midlothian
Waverley

PETER SHAFFER
The Royal Hunt of the Sun

WILLIAM SHAKESPEARE
A Midsummer Night's Dream
Antony and Cleopatra
As You Like It
Coriolanus
Cymbeline
Hamlet
Henry IV Part I
Henry IV Part II
Henry V
Julius Caesar
King Lear
Love's Labour's Lost
Macbeth
Measure for Measure
Much Ado About Nothing
Othello
Richard II
Richard III
Romeo and Juliet
Sonnets
The Merchant of Venice
The Taming of the Shrew
The Tempest
The Winter's Tale
Troilus and Cressida
Twelfth Night
The Two Gentlemen of Verona

GEORGE BERNARD SHAW
Androcles and the Lion
Arms and the Man
Caesar and Cleopatra
Candida
Major Barbara
Pygmalion
Saint Joan
The Devil's Disciple

MARY SHELLEY
Frankenstein

PERCY BYSSHE SHELLEY
Selected Poems

RICHARD BRINSLEY SHERIDAN
The School for Scandal
The Rivals

WOLE SOYINKA
The Lion and the Jewel
The Road
Three Short Plays

EDMUND SPENSER
The Faerie Queene (Book I)

JOHN STEINBECK
Of Mice and Men
The Grapes of Wrath
The Pearl

LAURENCE STERNE
A Sentimental Journey
Tristram Shandy

ROBERT LOUIS STEVENSON
Kidnapped
Treasure Island
Dr Jekyll and Mr Hyde

TOM STOPPARD
Professional Foul
Rosencrantz and Guildenstern are Dead

JONATHAN SWIFT
Gulliver's Travels

JOHN MILLINGTON SYNGE
The Playboy of the Western World

TENNYSON
Selected Poems

W. M. THACKERAY
Vanity Fair

DYLAN THOMAS
Under Milk Wood

EDWARD THOMAS.
Selected Poems

FLORA THOMPSON
Lark Rise to Candleford

J. R. R. TOLKIEN
The Hobbit
The Lord of the Rings

CYRIL TOURNEUR
The Revenger's Tragedy

ANTHONY TROLLOPE
Barchester Towers

MARK TWAIN
Huckleberry Finn
Tom Sawyer

VIRGIL
The Aeneid

VOLTAIRE
Candide

EVELYN WAUGH
Decline and Fall
A Handful of Dust

JOHN WEBSTER
The Duchess of Malfi
The White Devil

H. G. WELLS
The History of Mr Polly
The Invisible Man
The War of the Worlds

ARNOLD WESKER
Chips with Everything
Roots

PATRICK WHITE
Voss

OSCAR WILDE
The Importance of Being Earnest

TENNESSEE WILLIAMS
The Glass Menagerie

VIRGINIA WOOLF
To the Lighthouse

WILLIAM WORDSWORTH
Selected Poems

W. B. YEATS
Selected Poems